MOTHER GOD
and ME

OUR MEMOIRS

MOTHER GOD SPEAKS ABOUT THE UNIVERSE

THE STORY OF THE UNIVERSE

MOTHER GOD and LEN (URA) LA SCOLEA

with the witness: FELECIA (KLEA) LA SCOLEA

DEDICATION

This book is dedicated to the first author of this book, Mother God (Azna) herself. Who made it possible to communicate to me countless insights on The Spirit World and The Universe. A special recognition is to Felecia (Klea) La Scolea, The Witness in all this comprehensive communication with Mother God.

Acknowledgments

To three beautiful souls who have made this book a reality:
Rosemary Kristoff, my Consciousness from the beginning of this
Spiritual Journey of Klea and Ura. David Diomede with
his artistic gifts who made this book what it is.
Finally, to David Monroe Wright who was important in
the review process in writing this third book of
The Series of The Spiritual Journey of Klea and Ura.
Our Trilogy of the Spiritual Journey.

Mother God herself dictated what she wanted for the cover
of this book showing The Sword of Justice with a special
note of recognition to the artist Jolene Gentry.

Sometimes to Uncover What is Hidden
We Must First Be Made to Look

The Control Voice of the 1963 TV Series *The Outer Limits*

WHO BETTER TO ASK?

Since recorded history, humankind has thought of its place in the Cosmos and all the secrets within. There are a multitude of mysteries within our internal and external Universe. Who better to ask but our Co-Creator Mother God about the mysteries of the Universe? There is nothing better than going directly to the source.

I, URA, DID NOT WRITE THIS BOOK ALONE

There are two authors of this book. Mother God herself and I, Ura. The first author of this book is Mother God. The core of this book was written by Mother God. As her son, I have written parts of this book but the answers to 100 questions on the Universe and where this small planet called *Earth* stands in the cosmos was dictated to me by Mother herself. The answers will be beyond comprehension to many and shake others to their core of existence. There will be others though who will realize the omnipotent wisdom of her answers. This is not about belief, faith, feelings or opinions, it is about the truth across time in the Universe from the Co-Creator.

THIS IS THE FIRST TIME EVER IN THE HISTORY OF THIS PLANET THAT MOTHER GOD COMMUNICATED TO ALL OF US IN BOOK FORM.

URA

Contents

Prologue

ALL THESE REVELATIONS HAVE BEEN FORESEEN
FORETOLD BEFORE THE COMPLETION OF THE
UNIVERSE. WHEN ALL SOULS WERE IN THEIR
INCEPTION, BEFORE REMEMBRANCE.
A GREAT BATTLE WILL OCCUR IN THE UNIVERSE
BETWEEN THE LIGHT AND THE DARKNESS.
A SPIRITUAL WARRIOR OF JUSTICE WILL
LEAD THE WARRIORS OF THE LIGHT.

MOTHER AND FATHER GOD

Author's Note

FAR OUT MAN

1990 American Comedy Film

You mean to tell me Len (Ura) you are actually in constant communication with Mother God our Co-Creator with Father God. The only thing I can say is FAR OUT MAN!!! Before you place me in a padded room, lock the door, and throw away the key, let us tell you our story from the beginning.

It started over two years ago with my very beautiful wife Felecia (Klea), who I thought had died from cancer on November 5, 2018. Needless to say I was a 'mess' in every way emotionally, physically, mentally, and spiritually. I didn't even know who I was anymore. I would have taken a bullet for her to keep her with me. I was broken. I would have done anything to keep my heart, my Felecia, with me.

I described in our first book titled: *For All Is Love: A Spiritual Journey of Eternal Love* with the description The Woman On The Other Side, The Man On This Side and Their Extraordinary Story of Determination to be Together; how I navigated through this nightmare in the early months of our journey. Being the ultimate skeptic about anything connected to the Afterlife, a colossal transformation took place. The many ways we learned to communicate with each other and learning about the numerous past lives we shared. What, Reincarnation you say!!! Before the colossal transformation Reincarnation was just a word. After Death Communication (ADC) not a chance. Being a Bronx boy, FUHGEDDABOUTIT!!! (a New York City endearment). The numerous transformational events that happened with our reaching out to each other across dimensions. Resulting with our daily communication on so many levels. Ending with the fact that nothing in this Universe will ever stop eternal love.

Our love story continued on in our second book titled: *Conversations With My Sweetheart On The Other Side* with the description The Autobiography of Klea, A Detailed Description of Life on The Other Side. The question was asked what immediately happened after Klea so called 'died'? What happened at the moment of her 'death'? WHAT LIFE WAS LIKE AFTER YOU DIE?

Through our forms of communication Klea told me about where she went, what she did, who she was with, and who she met. Klea revealed in great detail about the many Temples and Halls on The Other Side. She talked extensively about our Co-Creators, Mother and Father God.

Communication advanced to the point that I, Ura, was having a regular connection of communication with many on The Other Side, including Mother God. Are you telling me you were having constant communication with Mother God? The revelations Mother God was telling me about The Spirit Word and The Universe were nothing short of astounding.

Why this third book had to be written was because of the revelations Mother God was telling me about numerous aspects of The Universe. Mother God had to be the main author of this third book of the Spiritual Journey of Klea and Ura because it would have been impossible to write this third book without all the incredible information Mother God was telling me about The Spirit World and The Universe. This is our book, *Mother God and Me*. FAR OUT MAN AGAIN!!! We may never let you out of that padded room. Don't let this guy out into society. OK, let's go on this wild ride and see what Mother God is telling us about The Universe. Are you ready for the ride of your life?

CHAPTER 1

THE VOICE

As described in our first two books of Klea and I, Ura, we communicated first by Clairsentience right from the beginning, feeling that powerful spirit energy that went through me. Simply, nothing like it in life here on This Side. Then came the subjective Clairvoyance which became quite acute. The last spiritual gift of communication to develop was the Clairaudience to hear Klea's voice. All the focus was on the communication between Klea and Ura.

Do you remember the famous 1989 movie *Field of Dreams* starring Kevin Costner? In the movie all the focus is on bringing back 'Shoeless Joe Jackson' the famous baseball player of the 1919 Chicago White Sox who 'threw' the World Series with his teammates. 'Shoeless Joe' and several teammates were banned from playing baseball forever. Kevin Costner (or in the movie Ray Kinsella) hears THE VOICE in his cornfield in Iowa "IF YOU BUILD IT HE WILL COME"; "EASE HIS PAIN"; then finally at a Boston Red Sox baseball game "GO THE DISTANCE."

All the focus in the movie is to bring back 'Shoeless Joe' to play baseball again with his banned teammates from baseball on the baseball field Ray Kinsella built for them on his Iowa farm. Then at the very end of this great story, it was revealed it was always about building the baseball field and to ease the pain for his father, John, who died young on poor terms with his son, Ray. His Dad was a minor league baseball player. To bring back his Dad to play baseball on his son's Iowa baseball field and to ease the pain the way the father and son departed.

In many respects it was like this in our Spiritual Journey of Klea and Ura to communicate in so many ways all this time not thinking there may be a Greater Focus, a Greater Purpose that was later revealed in our Spiritual Journey.

It was all about THE VOICE I started to hear about 8 months ago. A distinct female voice from The Other Side, The Spirit World, The Universe. Was this journey all along about the communication with Mother God and then Father God to me? Was this the Main Focus all along? To have the awakening of my real identity, which was hidden through all the ages by Mother and Father God, that I was their son for my protection from The Darkness. To only have Mother and Father God know this through the eons of time.

As you read this book, the last of the Trilogy of the Spiritual Journey of Klea and Ura, FOCUS ON THE ANSWERS THAT MOTHER GOD GIVES ME TO THE 100 QUESTIONS ON *EARTH* and THE UNIVERSE and ASK YOURSELF ONE SIMPLE QUESTION:

WOULD I BE EVEN REMOTELY CAPABLE OF GIVING ANSWERS OF THIS NATURE?

CHAPTER 2

MY RELATIONSHIP TO MOTHER AND FATHER GOD

INDICATIONS OF A SPECIAL RELATIONSHIP

There were many indications cited that I had a real close relationship to Mother and Father God, which I simply now call the 24 Questions to Mother. I missed all these indications until I started to ask numerous questions directly to Mother God:

1 – As explained in detail in Book 2, the process of the indications in my relationship to the Godhead, Mother and Father God started with when my beautiful Klea returned to The Other Side often called HOME. After an incarnation a soul returns HOME and during the process meets with their own Council of Elders in the Hall of Justice to review the past life that was completed. There is a comprehensive evaluation of this past life just finished to decipher if the soul accomplished all their objectives in the learning of lessons to advance their soul spirituality. The Council of Elders started to talk to Klea about Ura and how he was very important and powerful. Klea asked herself why is her own Council of Elders talking about Ura?

2 – The Council of Elders never visit the private homes of people. It is unheard of. The Council of Elders made two visits to our home that Klea has prepared for us. Several Council Members came. They talked about before Ura incarnated in this present life there were situations that required someone to stand up for what was good, justice, love and to be strong and Ura did it because it was the right thing to do. The Council of Elders hold Ura in high esteem. The Council Members had the knowing that I, Ura, was important but never knew how important till later.

3 – A complete chapter in Book 2 was devoted to this unique very powerful energy that Ura possesses that pierces and penetrates through everything on The Other Side. This has been described by so many on The Other Side, when I have power meditations with all my five Spirit Guides, numerous Council of Elders and angels who are present and Klea. All have never experienced this all powerful energy with the exception of the angels and the Presence, that flows through me when all step into my energy field. It has been stated by many my energy field is huge.

Now as previously described, The Presence located in The Hall of Justice above and behind The Council of Elders, with its white, violet, silver light shining down; I would merge my energy with the powerful energy of The Presence. I was told by everyone on The Other Side, The Presence actually started to change all kinds of colors and was actually 'sparking' it was so powerful. Nobody merges their energy with The Presence but I do; but what shocked those there was The Presence was merging its energy back to me. This was never seen or heard of before.

Why, I, Ura, have this gift of incredible powerful energy? This was a gift with a purpose. An energy that could reach across dimensions. That would have such an impact with so many on The Other Side. Furthermore the angels actually very much enjoyed the merging of Ura's energy.

The only plausible explanation is this energy originated from Mother and Father God. This was a gift with a purpose. What was the purpose? I, Ura, am a conduit for Mother and Father's love energy that flows through me. It is a great communion of love with Mother and Father God. An all powerful energy from the Godhead of love. This overwhelming energy that flows through me. I, Ura, ask what is the reason for this gift given to me by Mother and Father God?

4 – In my meditations I asked Mother God to cheer up Klea. The next day in our time Mother God came to visit Klea and in our home and told her everything will be fine. Just don't worry. Azna waved her sword and Klea immediately felt much better. When Mother God came to visit, Klea was shocked. This doesn't happen. It is all because of Ura.

5 – Klea and Ura were given over a short time incredible rare gifts of communication. What has been described extensively in both prior books, the gift of Clairsentience, to feel powerful waves of energy merging within Klea and Ura in so many different ways. This gift of Clairsentience was present early in the spiritual journey of Klea and Ura. It developed into a magnificent form of communication. Then came the subjective Clairvoyance, the ability to see Klea. Finally, what developed last was the Clairaudience, the ability to hear each other. Hearing each other became highly powerful and accurate. In such a short time why were Klea and Ura given these three rare incredible gifts of communication when so many who have devoted their entire life to the Afterlife don't have this blessing? Now these communication gifts have expanded to the interaction with all five Spirit Guides, Angels, and Council members, and finally to Mother God herself.

6 – My Master Spirit Guide (MSG) describes that I always had five Thrones around me that have recently increased dramatically in numbers. The Thrones are Mother God's personal army of angels. This simply does not happen with other souls during an incarnation.

7 – As well as my walking away from several outrageous situations of certain death like nothing happened in this incarnation.

8 – Klea, Spirit Guides, Council Members all HEAR Mother God talking to me. The dialogue between Mother and I is constant.

9 – Finally, there are the 24 questions to Mother I asked her in which it would be a total impossibility of myself in knowing any of this information in which she states right off that I, Ura am her son with Father God. Actually her son, not symbolic but actually their son. I was chosen based on my soul characteristics before the completion of the Universe for tasks which were designed for me. After going through several stages of disbelief I accepted this phenomenal revelation being told countless times by Mother herself.

COMMUNICATION WITH MOTHER GOD

Now what is the nature of our communication between Mother and I? First, how Mother and Father God communicate with us is by a voice in our mind but not in our mind, in our head but not in our head. Bilocation of a soul is that one can be in two places at the same time. It has to do with dividing up the soul energy. All souls can learn to do bilocation. Higher, more evolved souls, can be in multiple locations at once. For Mother and Father God there is an infinite number of places they can be at the same time. Mother and Father are everywhere and can take on any form they choose.

As mentioned I talk to her constantly mostly out loud but sometimes in my mind. She always answers directly right to the point with a strong touch of caring and love, like a Mother should. Mother has a very distinctive female voice. It is strong and loving every time. I will ask her questions and she immediately answers. It is a very caring voice. It is certainly not my voice. One knows their own voice in your thoughts, in your head. It is certainly not me with a female voice in my head. Plus, she gives information I would never be aware of and uses phrases I simply would never use. One knows their own thoughts in their head.

I added a disclaimer to our last book stating people are never going to believe this. I am certainly not crazy and not hearing things and voices in my head. I am certainly not having auditory hallucinations.

Mother and I communicate continuously and she says she is always there for me, which she is. We are always talking like a mother to a son, and a son to a mother. Mother and I have such strong bonds. Mother communicates with me on several levels, the conscious mind, the subconscious mind, images, telepathic pathways of thoughts. It is an astounding bond of communication. **IT IS INSTANTANEOUS COMMUNICATION**. She will do what I call 'Mother's nudges'. Whether I am awake or asleep she will place an idea or information in my mind and I just smile knowing it is her. She has a great sense of humor and we laugh all the time. I marvel often at how beautiful these bonds of communication are. I have been blessed beyond any measurement. We are so close that if I have specific thoughts and get very emotional she gets emotional too, and in the reverse if she gets emotional, I feel it and get emotional too. Especially when I think about the horrible 15 months to save Felecia (Klea) and keep her here with me in this dimension. Remember everything is blocked off by the amnesia blocks, so the only thoughts I have is in my conscious mind. The information in the subconscious mind is totally blocked off. Thus, these thoughts of the 15 month battle with cancer for Felecia (Klea) is all the thoughts I have to work with. Mother and I have this eternal, unbreakable bond that is an incredible blessing.

COMMUNICATION WITH FATHER GOD

Now there are countless references in history when Father God speaks to you. It is a very strong, powerful male voice in your head but not in your head. A voice of sheer maleness. An acute omnipotent intelligence of few words but to the point as with Mother's communications. You can feel the love of Father as with Mother, communication with both is a humbling and exhilarating experience beyond any description.

As described in our last book, it was November 5, 2020 at 1:35 am. At the time it was lost to me of the significance of this date: It was the second anniversary of my beautiful Klea going HOME. While Father God was communicating with me, this fact was lost to me, maybe because I was so stunned by the event. However, as I write this I am still shocked by this powerful synchronicity.

The setting of this direct communication with Father God was: I was working into the night as I often do on my computer in the dining room. For some unexplained reason I say out loud "How am I doing?" To this day I have no idea why I said this out loud.

Then a very powerful voice spoke to me in my head but not in my head and said:

You are doing fine my son. You were chosen long ago to be one of my soldiers. No one, nothing can harm you. I have tasks for you.

The voice came from outside my head but then in my head. My first reaction was I was totally stunned. I never would talk like that. I know my voice in my head. This was not my voice. This never happened before, ever. This voice certainly did not come from me. At the time I was on the computer thinking of other things. The contents of this message was the furthest thing from my mind. I would have never thought to say *"You were chosen long ago to be one of my soldiers."* I never would phrase a message like that. I don't think or talk like that. In a few sentences everything was answered.

It was a very strong, male voice, a very powerful message with great intelligence. I know the tenor of my voice in my head and how I phrase things. This most certainly was not my inner voice. This was not me. Father God sought me out to directly send me this message.

As previously mentioned in our last book, on The Other Side there are several locations of domes of communication with Father God where one can go. This was not on The Other Side in a dome of communication with Father God. It was right here on This Side in my dining room of our home. After a while still stunned and in shock, I lay in bed thinking and thinking about this direct communication with Father God.

Repeating and repeating over in my mind *"You were chosen long ago to be one of my soldiers. I have tasks for you."*

This briefly describes my special relationship as dictated by Mother and Father God. If anyone would have said to me all the revelations and experiences that happened with the spiritual journey of Klea and I and then the Celestial relationship with Mother and Father God three years ago, I simply would have asked "Have you totally lost your mind?"

Now Mother God had additional plans for our Celestial relationship. Mother took me higher and higher as described in the next chapter.

CHAPTER 3

THE CLAIRSENTIENCE OF MOTHER GOD

Why this third book had to be written was because of the revelations Mother God was telling me about numerous aspects of The Universe. Mother God had to be the main author of this third book of the Spiritual Journey of Klea and Ura because it would have been impossible to write this third book without all the incredible information Mother God was telling me about The Spirit World and The Universe. This is our book, *Mother God and Me*. **FAR OUT MAN AGAIN!!!** We may never let you out of that padded room. Don't let this guy out into society. OK, let's go on this wild ride and see what Mother God is telling us about The Universe. Are you ready for the ride of your life?

There are three major psychic gifts:

1) Clairsentience: the ability to feel or sense the energy of spirit
2) Clairvoyance: the inner sense of seeing as expressed through the mind's eye, the third eye or sixth Chakra
3) Clairaudience: the inner sense of hearing or better to listen

Clairsentience is like humidity: one cannot see or hear it, but you can sure feel it. Clairsentience was described extensively in our first two books. When I first began meditating in the early months of our journey together my Klea came through for the first time by very powerful waves of energy that literally 'rocked' my total body. The waves of spirit energy were so powerful they took on the tangible property of feeling solid. In this early stage, I only experienced these waves of energy when I had thoughts and images of Klea. With thoughts or images of anything other than Klea there was nothing. At first I had no idea what these powerful waves of energy were. After research and asking those in the Afterlife fields, I realized, it was the experience of feeling the energy of spirit, Clairsentience. Once you have the incredible joy to experience Clairsentience there is nothing like it in life. This amazing experience has always been constant, steady and strong from the beginning to the present in our journey.

Our Clairsentience evolved over time to what I called Target Clairsentience as described extensively in our first book. Where I would ask Klea out loud "to merge within me: total blending of our being, big hug, hold hands, in bed spoon with me, touch my heart," always at that moment I would feel powerful waves of love energy at that specific anatomical location. The response was always 100% every time I asked. Our Clairsentience in our first book became a confirmation tool to confirm what I was seeing by Clairvoyance, dates, letters, names, locations in the development of our Reincarnation Chart of the past lives Klea and I shared together. Stating out loud each letter, date, number if yes I would ask for a Clairsentience Blast, and nothing was simply a no. Still today as I write this now our Clairsentience is as strong and constant as ever. It has always been the one constant in our spiritual journey. A blessing beyond description.

Our Clairsentience continued to be utilized in different ways as described in our second book. It became the confirmation tool for our Clairaudience which was the last to develop of the three psychic gifts. Now our Clairaudience is very strong and accurate approaching 100%.

In our second book, Klea was describing in great detail what life was like on The Other Side. I was like a Court Reporter or Stenographer writing down what she was telling me by Clairaudience. Then asking her to confirm the accuracy by a Clairsentience blast if correct, yes and no being nothing. These descriptions of the highest Astral realm became like verbatim transcripts. The process was very rigorous confirming and reconfirming by Clairsentience Blasts. I have already been doing this for a long time with Klea, extensively described in our second book, *Conversations With My Sweetheart On The Other Side.*

Mother kept telling me for weeks she was going to show me some other things. It was Wednesday March 31, 2021 at 12:20 PM, a date and time I will never forget as long as I am still here on This Side. I was upstairs in the study opening my Chakras with simultaneous psychic exercises for enhancement of my Clairaudience and Clairvoyance within my mind not aided by any tapes, music etc. Just totally within my mind, a daily procedure.

Mother placed in my mind that she can give me Clairsentience as Klea and I do all the time. She only infused this in my mind just once. After the meditation I stood up and I talked to her out loud which is constant, continuous 24/7. "You can give me a Clairsentience Blast?" (which as you know is waves of energy going through your body).

Mother said, "Of course I can." By the tone in her voice I sensed she was kind of insulted by me questioning her on this. I mean after all she is Mother God. She asked, do you want me to and of course I said yes. I asked Mother four times and each time I received a strong Clairsentience Blast throughout my complete body. It 'rocked me'. I should have been sitting. Klea's Clairsentience is more local. Mother's Clairsentience is throughout my whole body. Like throughout my total being.

Now as I described in our second book how the communication with Mother God is an incredibly close bond of communication at all levels of consciousness, the subconscious, conscious mind, images, telepathically, infusion of information into my subconscious mind. She will do what I call 'Mother's Nudges'. Whether I am sleeping or awake, Mother will infuse information or ideas into my subconscious/conscious mind and I will smile because I know it is her. I become quickly aware it is her. I have become acutely sensitive to her thoughts to me.

Mother is so impressed how I 'pick things up' so quickly. She only told me once. Mother says to me you are a very exceptional soul. After this life changing experience what do you say to something like this? Just imagine I am merging my soul energy with Mother God. We are blending our energy together. Let that sink in for a moment. FAR OUT MAN!!! Get that padded room ready. I am totally astonished and shocked to say the least.

I went downstairs to the dining room where my computer is and started to document this as I always do with all experiences from the beginning of our journey. I was sitting and writing this out and asked Mother to give me another Clairsentience blast. Wow she almost 'knocked me' off my chair.

In talking to Klea as I am writing this, Klea is saying (verbatim) "I cannot believe this. It is amazing baby, totally!!!"

This just strengthens our bonds between Mother and I; if that is at all possible. I cannot conceive it being any closer. I am speechless. I am totally astonished. What do you say to something like this?

There are no words to describe the magnitude of this. I, Ura, son of Mother and Father God, sharing my soul energy with Mother God herself. There are no descriptions in feeling or words to describe something of this magnitude. This is a blessing beyond comprehension.

Klea is telling me as she is standing next to me as I am sitting typing on the computer all kinds of exclamations of amazement. The Clairsentience with Mother was totally unexpected. Mother and I, our bonds are so close she says something to me once and I know. It is just a knowing.

It has been called Claircognizance. Mother tells me she and Father are so proud of me that I am turning out much better than they even anticipated. They did not expect this. We are so anxious to take you HOME son. Mother tells me to get used to our Clairsentience because we will do it always. Mother told me several times that I have to accept the fact that I am a very exceptional soul. This Mother God Clairsentience experience was totally unexpected. Klea and I have to process this and revisit.

Now comes Part 2 of this amazing experience of Mother God's Clairsentience. Shortly thereafter I open my Chakras with a different method and at the end I speak out loud to those on The Other Side who are present that I can see by my Clairvoyance:

- my five spirit guides
- several types of angels
- council members from my own council (one woman and two men and several other council members)
- The Presence
- my beautiful Klea in white flowing robes
- the tall glowing profile of Mother God

I ask them to step into my energy field based on what I am saying, the merging of energy is powerful and sensational. This method I do every day. On that day I announced to everyone present on The Other Side that Mother God and I shared Clairsentience. We merged our love energy.

CHAPTER 3

After this meditation was finished, Carl, my Master Spirit Guide (MSG) came into the family room to talk to me as I was sitting in the recliner chair with Klea.

THE STATEMENT BY MY MSG

I have been a Spirit Guide for a very long time. I have never seen or heard of Mother God merging her energy of Clairsentience with any one with, of course, the exception of Father God. This is unbelievable. I simply don't know what to say. Mother God does not merge her energy with any one with the exception of Father God. My Spirit Guide team, especially Erica and Olivia, were so excited exclaiming to Ura; I heard them say to Ura this is so exciting, they needed 'time' to process this. Mother God does not merge her energy with any council member. The council members present were astonished. They have never heard of such a thing.

YOU ARE TRULY HER SON!!!

One day later, I, Ura, asked Mother about the merging of our energy through Clairsentience and the far reaching effects.

Mother stated (verbatim): "In the matrix of consciousness of the Universe, all souls immediately are connected with communication. All The Other Sides of the inhabited planets now know of this merging of our energy and are astonished by this. This event had a very positive effect on all the other planets of the Universe. Son, this is the beginning of many loving events that will transform the Universe. So many spirits on all these planets are anxious to meet you. Yes, now they know you are truly my son."

Also critical to this far reaching event that is unprecedented in the Universe is when Mother speaks to me, I can confirm my Clairaudience of what she says to me with a Clairsentience confirmation or blast. As I write this I am still astonished by the magnitude of this event.

CHAPTER 4

THE DAYS OF MARCH AND APRIL

I am not sure how this all started. Our second book was just published on Amazon. We had a great sense of achievement of completing this task. I thought now for some down time. I can relax for awhile. I am not sure if Mother was giving me one of her consciousness 'nudges' or it actually came from me. Wait a minute as I am writing this to you Mother just told me she was 'nudging' me to start asking many more questions. I had the 24 questions to Mother in the second book but now she wanted me to ask many more questions. There is no limit to how I marvel at the diversity of the communication bonds between Mother and I. Mother to a son and a son to a Mother. There is no limit to our love for each other.

Based on Mother's 'nudges' I started to ask questions in earnest, 'in a flurry' on so many topics about the Universe and the Spirit World. The answers from Mother, verbatim, were instantaneous and rigorously confirmed and reconfirmed and then confirmed by a Clairsentience Blast. Maybe that is why she wanted to develop our Clairsentience relationship to use it as a confirming process to everything Mother was telling me by Clairaudience. Mother just told me that was her thinking. She wanted to use Clairsentience to confirm everything she was telling me. Exactly what Klea and I were doing for quite awhile. Mother again just told me I am so fast at "picking things up." Father and I are so impressed with you. Mother and I, our communication is instantaneous every moment of existence. I cannot begin to describe how magnificent all this comprehensive communication is.

Mother and I communicate by Clairaudience and Clairsentience. Now the only major form of psychic communication remaining between Mother and I is Clairvoyance. Although I do see her tall glowing profile many times during the day. Mother never ceases to amaze me. What am I thinking, Len, she is Mother God. Get hold of yourself already. It is not everyday one communicates constantly with Mother God.

THE WITNESS

The following chapters are classified by topic. I ask Mother God questions she gives me answers, verbatim and with rigorous confirmation. The SILENT WITNESS in this complete process is my beautiful Klea, my twin soul, who has remarked countless times in utter amazement of the communication between Mother and I. Klea stands next to me and hears everything. Every time I get Mother's Clairsentience Blast as confirmation of what she is telling me, Klea sees my reaction. The questions and answers cover a lot of ground but it will never be complete because the questions can be just about endless when speaking about the Universe and The Spirit World. So let us embark upon this exciting, amazing Journey of Mother God herself telling this world here, This Side, about the Universe we all live in. Here we go for the ride of your life.

WHAT COMES FORTH IS THE STORY OF THE UNIVERSE AS TOLD BY OUR CO-CREATOR, MOTHER GOD. HER OMNIPOTENT WORDS OF WISDOM ARE SACRED. WE ARE ALL HER CHILDREN AND LOVED UNCONDITIONALLY. THE MAGNITUDE OF THESE WORDS, THE KNOWLEDGE, WILL ECHO IN YOUR CONSCIOUSNESS FOR ALL ETERNITY.

CHAPTER 5

THE SOUL AND CONSCIOUSNESS

1 – *MOTHER, WHAT IS THE SOUL?*

THE SOUL, SON, IS THE TOTAL ENERGY, ESSENCE OF A SPIRIT BEING. IT IS WHO THEY REALLY ARE. IT IS THE 'POWERHOUSE' OF ENERGY FOR THE SPIRIT BEING. IT IS THEIR TOTAL ESSENCE. THE ENERGY OF THE SOUL COMES FROM FATHER AND I.

2 – *MOTHER, WHERE IS THE SOUL THAT IS CONNECTED TO OUR BODY BY THE ENERGY CORD?*

SON, THE SOUL IS JUST ABOVE THE HEAD OF THE BODY. THE ENERGY CORD CONNECTS TO THE BACK OF THE HEAD. THE ENERGY CORD IS AS LONG AS YOU NEED WHEN YOU HAVE ASTRAL VISITS TO HOME WHEN YOU SLEEP.

3 – *MOTHER, WHERE IS CONSCIOUSNESS?*

CONSCIOUSNESS SON IS EVERYWHERE THROUGH THE UNIVERSE. IT IS THROUGH AND AROUND ALL THINGS IN THE UNIVERSE. THE BRAIN RECEIVES ITS INSTRUCTIONS FROM CONSCIOUSNESS.

CONSCIOUSNESS PERMEATES THE BRAIN. THERE IS A VERY CLOSE ASSOCIATION BETWEEN CONSCIOUSNESS

AND THE BRAIN. IN NEAR DEATH EXPERIENCES THE BRAIN MAY NOT BE FUNCTIONING BUT CONSCIOUSNESS IS STILL THERE OF AWARENESS OF EVERYTHING IN THE SURROUNDING ENVIRONMENT. REMEMBER SINCE CONSCIOUSNESS IS EVERYWHERE IN THE UNIVERSE IT HAS AWARENESS OF THE OTHER SIDE.

4 – MOTHER, WHAT IS THE RELATIONSHIP OF THE SOUL TO CONSCIOUSNESS?

THEY ARE 'INTERMINGLED'. THEY PERMEATE THROUGH EACH OTHER. THEY CANNOT BE SEPARATED. THEY ARE INTERDEPENDENT ON EACH OTHER. THEIR ENERGIES IMMERSE WITHIN THEMSELVES. IT IS A 'MIXING' OF ENERGIES OF THE SOUL AND CONSCIOUSNESS.

5 – MOTHER, TELL ME ABOUT THE DIFFERENCES BETWEEN THIS TEMPORARY BODY ON THIS SIDE BUILT FOR ONE LIFE AND THE ETERNAL ASTRAL BODY ON THE OTHER SIDE.

SON, THE ASTRAL BODY IS ETERNAL WITH A HIGH DEGREE OF SUPERIOR OR GREATER MATTER. ITS MOLECULAR STRUCTURE IS VERY DENSE. THE ATOMS ARE ARRANGED IN SUCH A WAY TO ALWAYS RECEIVE THE FULL DIVINE ENERGY FROM FATHER AND I. ALL SOULS ARE ETERNAL FROM FATHER AND I. ALL SOULS ARE ETERNAL BECAUSE THEY ARE ALL PART OF FATHER AND I OUR MOLECULAR STRUCTURE.

THE BODY USED FOR ONE LIFE IS GREATLY INFERIOR MATTER, LOOSELY PUT TOGETHER. IT IS BUILT AS A DISPOSABLE BODY FOR A PERIOD OF TIME. THE MOLECULAR

STRUCTURE IN ARRANGEMENT OF THE ATOMS IS NOT ARRANGED IN A WAY TO RECEIVE THE DIVINE ENERGY FROM FATHER AND I. BECAUSE OF THIS, THE ATOMS THAT MAKE UP THE CELLS ARE SUSCEPTIBLE TO MANY DIFFERENT TYPES OF DISEASE.

THE ARRANGEMENT OF THE ATOMS DETERMINE THE RECEIVING OF FATHER AND I, OUR DIVINE ENERGY. IN THE INFERIOR MATTER THERE IS A GREAT SPACE BETWEEN THE ROTATING ELECTRONS AND THE NUCLEUS. WITH THE ASTRAL BODY THE ROTATING ELECTRONS ARE MUCH CLOSER TO THE NUCLEUS, CLOSING THAT MOLECULAR SPACE, MAKING THE ASTRAL BODY MUCH MORE DENSE.

6 – *MOTHER, CAN YOU EXPLAIN IN MORE DETAIL THE CHARACTERISTICS OF THE ETERNAL ASTRAL BODY.*

SON, THE ASTRAL BODY IS ETERNAL BECAUSE OUR (FATHER AND I) ENERGY IS TOTALLY IMMERSED WITHIN THE MOLECULAR STRUCTURE OF THE ASTRAL BODY. THROUGH ALL THE ATOMS. ALL SOULS ARE ALWAYS PART OF OUR MOLECULAR STRUCTURE SO THE CONNECTION IS ALWAYS THERE.

NOW THE ASTRAL BODY IS A *SIMULATION* OF THE BIOLOGICAL FUNCTIONS OF THE TEMPORARY BODY DURING INCARNATIONS. THE BODY FUNCTIONS ARE NOT NECESSARY LIKE BREATHING BECAUSE OUR (FATHER AND I) ENERGY SUPPORTS ALL THE BIOLOGICAL FUNCTIONS. THE FUNCTIONS ARE NOT NECESSARY BUT SOULS ARE USED TO THEM DURING INCARNATIONS SO WE KEEP

THEM BECAUSE THAT MAKES THEM MORE COMFORT-
ABLE. SOULS DON'T NEED TO BREATHE BUT THE *SIM-
ULATION* IS THERE. ALL THE ENERGY FOR ALL BODILY
FUNCTIONS ARE SUPPORTED BY FATHER AND I.

7 – MOTHER, WHAT DOES THE FETUS INHERIT?

SON, THE FETUS, THE GENETIC MATERIAL OF EVERY CELL
IS COMPOSED OF THE BIOLOGICAL MATERIAL FROM
THE MOTHER AND FATHER BUT ALSO EVERY SOUL THAT
INCARNATES HAS PART OF THE MOLECULAR STRUCTURE
OF FATHER AND I.

THUS, THE FETUS IS COMPOSED OF THE SOUL WHEN IT
INCORPORATES BUT ALSO THE MOLECULAR STRUCTURE
OF FATHER AND I PLUS THEN THE BIOLOGICAL GENET-
IC MATERIAL FROM THE FATHER AND MOTHER IN THAT
PRESENT INCARNATION. EVERY SOUL ALWAYS HAS PART
OF FATHER AND I. THE SOUL USUALLY COMES INTO THE
FETUS NEAR THE END. THERE IS NO PURPOSE FOR THE
SOUL TO COME INTO THE FETUS EARLY.

*8 – MOTHER, WHAT ARE THE CHARACTERISTICS OF THE
CONCEPT OF TIME ON THIS SIDE, THE OTHER SIDE, AND IN
THE UNIVERSE?*

SON, TIME ON YOUR SIDE IS LINEAR, PAST, PRESENT, AND
FUTURE. ON THE OTHER SIDE AND IN THE TOTAL UNI-
VERSE THERE IS NO TIME. IT IS A FOREVER ONGOING CON-
CEPT WHERE EVERYTHING IS OCCURRING ALL AT ONCE.
LIKE A CIRCLE, THERE IS NO END OR BEGINNING. FATHER
AND I WANTED SOULS TO NOT FEEL THE PRESSURE OF

TIME SO TIME BECAME A CONCEPT OF NON EXISTENCE. SO THE PAST IS STILL HAPPENING, THE PRESENT IS JUST THERE AND THE FUTURE HAS ALREADY OCCURRED. THIS WAY SOULS DON'T HAVE TO FEEL THE PRESSURE OF TRYING TO GET THINGS DONE IN A RUSH IMMEDIATELY.

TIME IS A CONCEPT ONLY ON YOUR SIDE: TO FEEL THE END OF A LIFE THERE WITH AGING AND THEN COMING HOME. TIME ON YOUR SIDE GIVES ORDER, ORGANIZATION TO THE SCHEME OF REINCARNATION THERE. YOU COMPLETE A LIFE THEN YOU RETURN HOME. WITH NO LINEAR TIME ON YOUR SIDE IT WOULD MAKE REINCARNATION, THE MEASUREMENT OF SPIRITUAL PROGRESS CHAOTIC. TIME TRAVEL ON YOUR SIDE IS NOT POSSIBLE BECAUSE IT WOULD INTERFERE WITH REINCARNATION.

9 – *MOTHER, CAN ONE HAVE ACCESS TO THE PAST AND FUTURE?*

YES, OF COURSE SON, YOU CAN GO TO THE HALL OF RECORDS AND OTHER PLACES ON OUR SIDE OR THE OTHER SIDE AND IMMERSE YOURSELF IN THE PAST OR FUTURE EVENTS BY PULLING OUT THE HOLOGRAM TAPES OR RECORDS AND EXPERIENCE THE EVENT IN FULL LIFE AGAIN. ONE HAS A LIVING EXPERIENCE AND KNOWLEDGE OF THE PAST AND THE FUTURE TO SEE THE GLORIOUS EVENTS THAT ARE COMING. MOST SOULS DON'T LOOK INTO THE FUTURE , MOST ARE INTERESTED IN THE PAST. TIME TRAVEL IS ALREADY AVAILABLE ON OUR SIDE. YOU MERGE YOUR ENERGY INTO THE CONTINUUM OF CONSCIOUSNESS TO REACH THE EVER PRESENT PAST OR

FUTURE. YOU TRAVEL THROUGH THE ENERGIES OF CON-
SCIOUSNESS TO REACH THE PAST OR FUTURE.

10 – *MOTHER, IS THE DATE AND TIME OF BIRTH DETERMINED PRIOR TO AN INCARNATION?*

YES SON, IT IS. IT INVOLVES ASTROLOGY OF THE POSI-
TION OF THE PLANETS AND SUNS. THE SOUL CHARAC-
TERISTICS DETERMINES WHEN A SOUL WILL ENTER YOUR
REALM. FOR INSTANCE, YOU ARE A VERY POWERFUL SOUL
WITH STRONG CHARACTERISTICS, SO THE ALIGNMENT
OF VARIOUS PLANETS AND SUNS HAS TO COINCIDE WITH
YOUR TRAITS AS A SOUL. IT IS THE RELATING OF A SOUL'S
TRAITS TO THE HEAVENLY ARRANGEMENT. WE LOOK AT
THE HEAVENLY ARRANGEMENT AND THAT COINCIDES
WITH THE SOUL TRAITS AND THAT IS THE TIME A SOUL
IS BORN. THE HOUR OF THE DAY IS ALSO LOOKED AT
AGAIN CORRESPONDING TO A SOUL CHARACTERISTICS.
THIS GIVES YOU A GENERAL IDEA. A BIRTH DATE IS NOT A
RANDOM EVENT.

11 – *MOTHER, TELL ME ABOUT THE BIRDS THAT KEEP FOL-
LOWING ME FOR SEVERAL DAYS AT THE WINDOWS OF OUR
HOME AND ARE ALWAYS PECKING AT THE WINDOWS FIRST
WHERE I WORK ON THE COMPUTER IN THE DINING ROOM
AND NOW WHEN I AM SITTING IN THE FAMILY ROOM, WHICH
HAS NEVER EVER HAPPENED BEFORE. IT IS VERY DRAMATIC.*

SON, IT IS A CONNECTION OF CONSCIOUSNESS. A LINK
IS MADE OF ENERGY BETWEEN THE BIRDS AND YOU;
CONSCIOUSNESS TO CONSCIOUSNESS. THIS ENERGY

LINK LASTS FOR A WHILE THEN WILL DISSIPATE. THE SPIRIT WARRIORS ELON and ARON WANTED TO MEET YOU RELATED TO THE TASKS AHEAD AND START TO PLAN, AS YOUR BROTHERS IN ARMS. THE BIRDS WERE USED TO GET YOUR ATTENTION. SO THEY CREATED AN ENERGY LINK BETWEEN THE BIRDS CONSCIOUSNESS AND YOU BY THE MANIPULATION OF THE ENERGY IN THE MATRIX OF CONSCIOUSNESS WITH ALL LIVING THINGS. IT IS JUST AN ENERGY LINK OF CONSCIOUSNESS. WHEN YOU RETURN HOME YOU WILL LEARN HOW TO MANIPULATE AND CONTROL CONSCIOUSNESS.

CHAPTER 6

INSIGHTS ABOUT MOTHER, FATHER GOD AND URA

1 – ALL SOULS ARE THE CHILDREN OF MOTHER AND FATHER GOD. MOTHER, WHAT MAKES ME SO SPECIAL?

BECAUSE SON, YOU WERE CHOSEN BEFORE THE COMPLETION OF THE UNIVERSE FOR SPECIAL TASKS. THAT IS WHAT MAKES YOU DIFFERENT FROM ALL THE OTHERS.

2 – MOTHER, HOW DO YOU AND FATHER COMMUNICATE?

WE ARE IN CONSTANT COMMUNICATION BY MERGING OUR ENERGIES. THUS, WHATEVER KNOWLEDGE IS AUTOMATICALLY SHARED.

3 – MOTHER, YOU AND FATHER ARE EVERYWHERE, HOW DO YOU DO THIS? I KNOW YOU HAVE AN INFINITY OF LOCATIONS YOU CAN BE AT THE SAME TIME, HOW?

BECAUSE WE BOTH PERMEATE THE FIELD OF CONSCIOUSNESS IN THE UNIVERSE. WE SATURATE CONSCIOUSNESS IN THE UNIVERSE.

4 – WE SOULS TAKE ON HUMAN FORM HERE AS AN IMAGE OF YOU AND FATHER, PLEASE EXPLAIN.

SON, BECAUSE EVERY SOUL IN THE UNIVERSE HAS PART OF OUR MOLECULAR STRUCTURE, BOTH FATHER AND I. SO EACH SOUL RECEIVES PART OF ME AND FATHER FROM OUR MOLECULAR STRUCTURE. THAT IS THE GENERAL IDEA.

5 – MOTHER, YOU ARE PRIMARILY EMOTION AND SECOND-ARILY INTELLECT. WHEREAS FATHER IS INTELLECT AND SECONDARILY EMOTION. PLEASE EXPLAIN.

I CONCENTRATE ON EMOTION AS A MOTIVATOR FOR AC-TION. EMOTION IS A GREAT DRIVING FORCE FOR ACTION. FATHER CONCENTRATES ON INTELLECT TO MAINTAIN THE STABILITY OF THE UNIVERSE. FATHER HAS EMOTION BUT IT IS SUBDUED. SO WE COMPLEMENT EACH OTHER.

6 – MOTHER, WHY DO I HAVE TO RETURN HOME NOW?

BECAUSE THE NEEDS OF THE UNIVERSE ARE GREATLY MORE IMPORTANT THAN ONE PLANET. THIS WAS DE-SIGNED LONG AGO.

Mother and I constantly mention to each other how we enjoy our discussions so much. She constantly tells me when I return home and have my total mind back she will take me up to the Causal or Mental and Celestial realms to continue our discussions. There is so much beauty she wants to show me. Our discussions will always be with Father too.

7 – MOTHER, IN MY RESEARCH I LEARNED ABOUT AN ETER-NAL MARRIAGE CEREMONY. CAN YOU DESCRIBE THIS FOR ME.

YES SON, IT IS TOTALLY PERFORMED BY THE COUNCIL OF ELDERS. A COUPLE GOES TO THE COUNCIL OF ELDERS AND PETITIONS FOR A MARRIAGE. THE COUNCIL SETS UP ALL THE DETAILS. THE COUPLE CAN BE TWIN SOULS OR NOT. THE COUNCIL INTERVIEWS THE COUPLE AND DECIDES IF IT IS APPROPRIATE FOR THEM. IF THE COUNCIL AGREES WITH THE COUPLE A CEREMONY IS PERFORMED. IT IS A BEAUTIFUL LOVING CEREMONY. GUESTS ARE INVITED. THE COUPLE SAYS WORDS TO EACH OTHER. THE COUPLE IS UNITED FOR ALL ETERNITY. THERE ARE OTHER THINGS THAT ARE DONE, BUT THIS IS A GENERAL DESCRIPTION. MANY COUPLES HAVE THIS CEREMONY PERFORMED.

IF YOU AND KLEA DECIDE TO DO THIS I WILL BE PRESENT AND I AM SURE FATHER WILL SAY A FEW WORDS. SON, THIS IS A VERY GOOD THING FOR YOU. KLEA WILL GIVE YOU ETERNAL STABILITY AND LOVE. THAT IS WHY FATHER AND I SELECTED HER FOR YOU. THIS STABILITY AND LOVE WILL BE IMPORTANT FOR YOUR FRAME OF MIND FOR THE TASKS THAT AWAIT YOU. THERE WILL BE NO DISTRACTIONS. YOU HAVE TO BE FOCUSED SON FOR THE TASKS AHEAD.

I WILL BE READY MOTHER FOR THE TASKS THAT AWAIT ME. I WILL BE RESOLUTE.

I KNOW MY DEAR SON.

8 – *MOTHER, FATHER AND YOU HAVE RESPONSIBILITIES IN THE UNIVERSE WHAT ARE THEY?*

SON, I AM RESPONSIBLE FOR ALL THE INHABITED PLANETS OF THE UNIVERSE WHICH ARE MANY. FATHER IS RESPONSIBLE FOR THE STABILITY OF THE UNIVERSE. TO MAINTAIN THE UNIVERSE SO MATTER AND ENERGY DO NOT ENTER AN UNSTABLE STATE. FATHER HAS TO HOLD EVERYTHING TOGETHER. HE DOES THIS WITH AN ENORMOUS EXPENDITURE OF ENERGY. WITH MANY DIFFERENT FORMS OF ENERGY. THIS IS AN ETERNAL TASK. IF THIS IS NOT DONE THE UNIVERSE WOULD 'BREAK APART' AND EVERYTHING WOULD DISINTEGRATE.

9 – MOTHER TELL ME ABOUT THE FORMS YOU AND FATHER CAN TAKE.

SON, WE CAN TAKE ANY FORM WE CHOSE. FATHER PRIMARILY STAYS AND MAINTAINS SPIRIT FORM, HOWEVER HE DOES COME INTO PHYSICAL FORM ONLY RARELY. SINCE FATHER MUST MAINTAIN HIS ENERGY THROUGHOUT THE UNIVERSE TO KEEP IT INTACT. THAT IS WHY HE PRIMARILY STAYS IN SPIRIT FORM. THEN IT IS EASY TO BE EVERYWHERE.

I COME INTO PHYSICAL FORM OFTEN BECAUSE I HAVE TO ATTEND TO ALL THE INHABITED PLANETS AND IT REQUIRES INTERACTION WITH SOULS. THUS, I TAKE A PHYSICAL FORM. MY PHYSICAL FORM CAN VARY DEPENDING ON SITUATIONS.

10 – MOTHER, HOW WILL I RETURN HOME?

SON, I WILL TAKE YOUR HAND AND YOUR SOUL WILL

DETACH FROM YOUR BODY. THE ENERGY CORD WILL RELEASE FROM YOUR BODY. A BODY CANNOT SURVIVE WITHOUT A SOUL. YOU WILL THEN COME WITH ME HOME FOR ALL ETERNITY. THE CAUSE OF DEATH WILL BE CLASSIFIED AS NATURAL CAUSES.

CHAPTER 7

THE NATURE OF GOOD AND EVIL IN THE UNIVERSE

1 – MOTHER, WHAT ARE THE WHITE, GRAY, AND DARK ENTITIES IN THE UNIVERSE?

SON, THEY ARE THE THREE MAJOR TYPES OF SOULS IN THE UNIVERSE. THE WHITE ENTITIES ARE VERY LOVING, GIVING AND SERVE OTHERS. EVERYTHING IS BASED ON A SOUL'S ACTION DURING AN INCARNATION.

2 – MOTHER, WHY ARE THEY CALLED THE DARK, GRAY, AND WHITE ENTITIES?

SON, THIS HAS ABSOLUTELY NOTHING TO DO WITH SKIN COLOR. IT IS THE CORE COLOR ENERGY OF THEIR SOUL. THE DARK IS THE TOTAL ABSENCE OF LIGHT. THE GRAY HAVE 'DIM' LIGHT, AND THE WHITE ARE THE LIGHT OF LOVE.

3 – MOTHER, WHAT ARE THE DARK ENTITIES?

THESE ARE THE EVIL SOULS AS BASED ON THEIR ACTIONS DURING INCARNATIONS. THEY ARE CRUEL. EVERYTHING THEY DO IS TO BENEFIT THEMSELVES. THEY ONLY HAVE LOVE OF SELF. THEY ARE SUCCUMBED BY THE VICES OF

LOVE OF MONEY, GREED, POWER, AND DOMINANCE OVER OTHER SOULS. THEY SACRIFICE OTHER SOULS FOR THEIR BENEFIT. THEY ARE NEVER ALLOWED TO ENTER THE OTHER SIDE OF PLANETS THAT FATHER AND I CREATED. WHEN THEY DIE AS INCARNATE THEY ARE IMMEDIATELY MET BY THE CARRION ANGELS AT THE MOMENT OF DEATH AND TRANSFERRED BACK INTO INCARNATE FORM, INTO A FETUS.

4 – MOTHER, WHAT ARE THE GRAY ENTITIES?

THESE SOULS CANNOT BE TRUSTED AND ARE UNPREDICTABLE. THEY WANT ALL THE ADVANTAGES OF INCARNATION OF MONEY, POWER, VICES BUT ALSO AT TIMES WILL APPEAR TO BE SINCERE IN LOVING, GIVING, AND HELPING SERVING OTHERS; BUT IT IS ALL FALSE.

FATHER AND I PUT THEM INTO THE LOWEST ASTRAL PLANES. WE ALLOW THEM THE OPPORTUNITY TO CHANGE THEIR WAYS.

5 – MOTHER, WHAT ARE THE WHITE ENTITIES?

THEY ARE THE BEST SOULS FOR LOVE, GIVING, SERVING OTHERS, KINDNESS TO HELP OTHERS. THEY ARE FATHER AND I OUR 'PRIDE AND JOY'. THE WHITE ENTITIES HAVE TURNED OUT SO WELL. THEY ARE THE SOULS IN THE UNIVERSE THAT MUST BE PROTECTED AGAINST EVIL WHEN THEY INCARNATE. FATHER AND I WANT THEM TO LEARN ABOUT EVIL, BUT THEY MUST BE PROTECTED TOO.

6 – *MOTHER, HOW DID THE DARK ENTITIES EVOLVE, DEVELOP?*

LONG AGO THERE WERE SOULS WHO TURNED FROM THE LIGHT OF LOVE. THEY FELT THAT THEY KNEW BETTER THAN FATHER AND I. THEY SUCCUMBED, WERE SEDUCED BY THE EVIL OF VICES, CRUELTY, POWER, MORE POWER, GREED TO ONLY LOVE OF THEMSELVES. THE DARK ENTITIES TURNED AWAY FROM FATHER AND I. FATHER AND I KNEW THERE WOULD BE SOULS THAT WOULD BEHAVE THIS WAY. REMEMBER ALL SOULS HAVE FREE WILL IN THE UNIVERSE. THE DARK ENTITIES DETERMINED THEIR OWN FATE. THE DARK ENTITIES FELL FROM THE LIGHT.

7 – *MOTHER, TELL ME ABOUT THE DARK ENTITIES ON PLANET* EARTH?

SON, PLANET *EARTH* HAS THE HIGHEST PERCENTAGE OF DARK AND GRAY ENTITIES IN THE UNIVERSE. MUCH MORE THAN OTHER PLANETS. THE HIGHLY EVOLVED SOULS COME TO *EARTH* TO LEARN ABOUT THE DARK ENTITIES, TO LEARN ABOUT EVIL, AND HOW TO SURVIVE AMONG EVIL. THE ONLY WAY TO LEARN ABOUT EVIL IS TO EXPERIENCE IT AND TO SURVIVE EVIL.

8 – *MOTHER, ARE WE THE MOST EMOTIONAL PLANET IN THE UNIVERSE?*

YES, SON THAT IS CORRECT BECAUSE THERE IS SO MUCH EVIL THERE.

9 – *MOTHER, YOU MENTIONED* EARTH *HAS THE MOST DARK ENTITIES IN THE UNIVERSE, RELATIVE TO THE NUMBERS OF WHITE AND GRAY ENTITIES. DO THE DARK ENTITIES EXIST ANYWHERE ELSE IN THE UNIVERSE?*

YES SON, THEY ARE SCATTERED THROUGHOUT THE UNIVERSE BUT CONCENTRATE ON THEIR HOME PLANET CALLED *NOIR*. THERE ARE NO WHITE OR GRAY ENTITIES ON *NOIR*. THERE THEY ACTUALLY HAVE AN ORGANIZATION, A HIERARCHY. A PLANET THAT IS DEVOID OF LIGHT AND LOVE. THIS PLANET EXISTS BECAUSE OF FREE WILL IN THE UNIVERSE. THE PLANET *NOIR* EXISTS IN OUR DIMENSION BUT AT A MUCH LOWER VIBRATION FREQUENCY. IT IS A VERY DEPRESSING PLACE.

10 – *MOTHER, YOU SAID THE DARK ENTITIES HAVE A CENTRAL PLANET OF THEIR OWN CALLED* NOIR. *WHAT ABOUT THE WHITE ENTITIES DO THEY HAVE A PLANET OF THEIR OWN IN THE UNIVERSE?*

YES SON, IT IS CALLED *NUVO*. IT IS CENTRAL IN THE UNIVERSE WITH 7 RINGS AROUND IT. IT IS ALL WHITE AND A VERY BEAUTIFUL PLACE OF LIGHT. PEOPLE ACTUALLY LIVE ON THE RINGS. IT IS A PLACE OF HIGHLY EVOLVED SELECTED SOULS WHO WERE CHOSEN FOR A SPECIAL PURPOSE IN THE UNIVERSE TO HELP AND SAVE SOULS.

11 – *MOTHER, DO MY TASKS THAT AWAIT ME INVOLVE THE DARK ENTITIES' PLANET* NOIR?

YES SON, THIS IS A CENTRAL TASK FOR YOU AND THE SOLDIERS YOU WILL LEAD. *NOIR* IS THE CENTRAL CORE OF EVIL IN THE UNIVERSE. ITS REALITY CANNOT BE TOLERATED ANYMORE. IT HAS CAUSED TOO MUCH PAIN AND SUFFERING IN THE UNIVERSE. ITS EXISTENCE HAS TO BE ELIMINATED. MUCH DISCUSSION WILL OCCUR WHEN YOU COME HOME TO FATHER AND I IN THE CHOICES OF ELIMINATING THIS THREAT TO LOVE. SOULS MUST BE GIVEN THE OPPORTUNITY TO LOVE.

12 – MOTHER, HAS DARK POWERFUL ENERGY EMITTED FROM THE PLANET NOIR *AFFECTED CONSCIOUSNESS IN THE UNIVERSE?*

YES SON, IT HAS AFFECTED CONSCIOUSNESS IN A VERY NEGATIVE WAY, CAUSING SOULS MUCH PAIN AND SUFFERING IN THEIR MENTAL THOUGHTS. CAUSING MUCH ABUSE AND CRUELTY OF THOUGHTS TO WHITE ENTITIES. MUCH OF THE ADDICTIONS AND CRUEL ACTIONS DERIVE FROM THE SOURCE OF THE EVIL DARK ENERGY EMITTING FROM *NOIR* IN THE UNIVERSE, UNDERMINING THE PURITY OF CONSCIOUSNESS.

MOTHER, what you are really saying is Consciousness must be pure in the Universe.

ABSOLUTELY SON.

13 – MOTHER, IS IT POSSIBLE FOR SOUL ENTITIES TO BE DESTROYED OR A DEATH OF A SOUL CAN OCCUR?

NO SON, SOULS ARE ETERNAL AS FATHER AND I, IN OUR IMAGE. HOWEVER, A SOUL CAN BE DAMAGED OR SCARRED IN THE TRANSITION PROCESS HOME, BY ILLNESS OR VERY TRAUMATIC EXPERIENCES. AT THIS POINT WE PLACE THEM IN HEALING CENTERS TO RESTORE THEIR SOUL ENERGY. A SOUL CAN ONLY CEASE TO EXIST IF FATHER AND I REABSORB THEIR ENERGY.

14 – *MOTHER, THIS EXTREMELY POWERFUL HIGH VIBRATING ENERGY FROM THE CELESTIAL REALM THAT FLOWS THROUGH ME FROM YOU AND FATHER AND IS CONDUCTED THROUGH A SWORD, WILL THIS REABSORB THE SOUL ENERGY OF THE DARK ENTITIES?*

ABSOLUTELY SON, IN THE GREAT BATTLE YOUR SWORD WILL ELIMINATE THE SOUL ENERGY OF THE DARK ENTITIES. THEY WILL CEASE TO EXIST. JUST BY TOUCHING ANY PART OF THEM THEIR SOUL ENERGY WILL EVAPORATE. THIS IS FOR ALL DARK ENTITIES. THE DARK ENTITIES WILL VANISH FROM THE UNIVERSE.

15 – *MOTHER, THE WARRIORS OF THE LIGHT I WILL LEAD IN THE GREAT BATTLE WILL THEY ALSO HAVE SWORDS OF JUSTICE?*

YES SON, BUT YOURS WILL BE THE MOST POWERFUL. YOURS WILL BE THE ALL CONSUMING ENERGY. THEIR ENERGY WILL BE VERY EFFECTIVE BUT YOURS WILL BE TOTAL DESTRUCTION IN WHATEVER DARK ENTITY YOU ENCOUNTER.

16 – *MOTHER, WHY WAS THE EARTH CHOSEN AS THE MOST CHALLENGING PLANET IN THE UNIVERSE?*

BECAUSE SON, WE, FATHER AND I, NEEDED A PLACE FOR THE MOST EVOLVED SOULS TO RAPIDLY PROGRESS TO A MUCH HIGHER LEVEL OF SPIRITUALITY. FATHER AND I WANTED AN ADVANCED SCHOOL FOR LESSONS TO BE LEARNED BY THE WHITE ENTITY SOULS. *EARTH* IS THE MOST CHALLENGING, MOST DIFFICULT SCHOOL IN THE UNIVERSE.

17 – *MOTHER, WE HAVE MUCH DISEASE HERE ON EARTH. AS THE MOST CHALLENGING PLANET, WHAT ABOUT THE OTHER INHABITED PLANETS OF THE UNIVERSE?*

EARTH HAS THE HIGHEST DEGREE OF DISEASE COMPARED TO THE OTHER PLANETS BECAUSE THERE IS MUCH EVIL HERE AND THE SACRIFICE OF HUMAN LIFE. THE OTHER PLANETS HAVE SYSTEMS IN PLACE TO CARE FOR EVERYONE. IT IS A COMMUNITY OF CARE AND LOVE ON THE OTHER PLANETS. MANY HUMAN BEINGS HAVE BEEN SACRIFICED EXHIBITED BY DISEASE FOR SELFISH, EVIL, HUMAN INTENT.

18 – *MOTHER, TELL ME ABOUT ABORTION?*

SON, IT IS A TERRIBLE, TERRIBLE THING. THE FETUS IS CREATED BY FATHER AND I AND THEN DESTROYED BY SOULS ON YOUR SIDE. THE SOUL WILL NEVER ENTER A FETUS THAT IS PLANNED ON BEING DESTROYED. ABORTION IS FOR THE CONVENIENCE OF SOULS THERE. IT IS AN

EVIL PRACTICE. IT DOES NOT AFFECT THE SOUL BECAUSE A SOUL WILL NEVER ENTER A FETUS THAT IS SCHEDULED FOR AN ABORTION. PLUS, THE SOUL ENTERS THE FETUS LATE IN A PREGNANCY SO IT IS A NON ISSUE.

Let me add when I asked Mother this question I could feel how emotional and upset she was. Remember as mentioned earlier Mother and I are extremely bonded in communication on so many levels.

19 – *MOTHER, WHY DO BABIES AND CHILDREN DIE?*

SON, THEY DIE BECAUSE IT IS PLANNED BEFORE THEY TAKE A LIFE HERE THAT THERE HAS TO BE A COMPLETION OF SPIRITUAL LESSONS TO FINALIZE THEIR SPIRITUAL GROWTH. THEY ARE USUALLY VERY ADVANCED SOULS WHO ARE NEAR THE END OF THEIR LEARNING EXPERIENCE IN THEIR SPIRITUALITY. IT IS A HEARTBREAKING EXPERIENCE FOR THE PARENTS. FATHER AND I UNDERSTAND THIS BUT IT IS THE PROCESS OF COMPLETING THEIR SPIRITUALITY. WHEN THEY RETURN HOME IT IS USUALLY THEIR LAST INCARNATION AS A VERY ADVANCED SOUL. IT IS COMPLETING THE PROCESS OF THEIR SOUL GROWTH OR DEVELOPMENT. ON RETURNING HOME THEY THEN COMPLETE THE AGING PROCESS TO MATURITY.

20 – *MOTHER, WHY DO MISCARRIAGES OCCUR?*

SON, MISCARRIAGES ARE A MUST EVENT IN THAT THE PURPOSE OF THE SOUL IS TO LEARN LESSONS WHILE IN AN INCARNATION. IF CIRCUMSTANCES CHANGE THAT THE SOUL CANNOT LEARN THOSE LESSONS WHETHER

BY FAMILY CONDITIONS, HEALTH REASONS, OR OTHER CIRCUMSTANCES, THE SOUL LEAVES THE FETUS. THE FETUS CANNOT SURVIVE WITHOUT THE SOUL. IT IS A MUST SITUATION BECAUSE NOTHING CAN PREVENT THE SOUL FROM HAVING A REASONABLE CHANCE OF LEARNING ITS LESSONS.

21 – *MOTHER, WHAT IS THE VIEW REGARDING DRINKING ALCOHOL AND TAKING DRUGS, RELATED TO SERIOUS ADDICTIONS?*

SON, THESE SITUATIONS CREATE AN ATMOSPHERE WHERE THE SOUL CAN GET 'POISONED', IMPAIRING THE SOUL DURING AN INCARNATION. MUCH OF THIS IS THE EFFECT OF THE DARK ENTITIES ON THE SOUL 'POISONING' THE MIND OF THE SOUL DURING AN INCARNATION. AS A 'POISONED' SOUL, IT DOES NOT HAVE A CHANCE TO COMPLETE ITS LESSONS TO BE LEARNED DURING AN INCARNATION. THIS IS VIEWED AS A VERY NEGATIVE SITUATION DRAMATICALLY EFFECTING THE SPIRITUAL ADVANCEMENT OF THE SOUL. ALCOHOL AND DRUG ADDICTIONS MUST BE AVOIDED AT ALL COSTS, BECAUSE IT NUMBS THE SOUL OF ITS ENERGY. IT IMPAIRS THE ENERGY OF THE SOUL.

IF THE SOUL DIES OF AN ALCOHOL OR DRUG ADDICTION, THEY ARE IMMEDIATELY PLACED IN A HEALING CENTER TO RESTORE THE ENERGY OF AN IMPAIRED, 'POISONED' SOUL. IT IS A MAJOR SET BACK IN THE ADVANCEMENT OF THE SPIRITUALITY OF THE SOUL. MANY OF THESE SOULS ARE WHITE ENTITIES WHO HAVE A MAJOR SET BACK IN THEIR ADVANCEMENT OF THEIR SOUL SPIRITUALITY.

THE DARK ENTITIES UNDERMINING CONSCIOUSNESS IS A WAY THE MIND OF THE INDIVIDUAL GETS 'POISONED'.

22 – *MOTHER, WHAT IS THE VIEWPOINT ON SUICIDE?*

SON, THIS IS A VERY SERIOUS SITUATION IN THAT THE SOUL NEVER HAD A CHANCE TO COMPLETE LEARNING ITS LESSONS FOR THE SOUL ADVANCEMENT IN SPIRITUALITY. BECAUSE THE LESSONS WERE NOT COMPLETED, THE SOUL MUST RETURN TO AN INCARNATION AGAIN FACING A SIMILAR SITUATION IN WHICH THE SOUL TRIED TO ESCAPE. THE SOUL IS PLACED BACK IN AN INCARNATION IMMEDIATELY IN THE UNIVERSE. IT DOES NOT HAVE TO BE *EARTH*, BUT MOST OF THE TIME IT IS BECAUSE *EARTH* HAS THE GREATEST CHALLENGES. PLUS, THEIR LIFE CHART IS A CONTRACT WITH FATHER AND I. THIS CONTRACT HAS BEEN BROKEN AND A PERFECTLY GOOD BODY HAS BEEN WASTED.

23 – *MOTHER, WHAT IS THE VIEWPOINT ON ASSISTED SUICIDE?*

SON, THIS ALSO IS NOT GOOD. THE RESPONSIBILITY FOR A LIFE IS IN THE HANDS OF FATHER AND I. THIS IS LIKE THE SOUL IS 'PLAYING GOD'. IF THIS DOES OCCUR THE SOUL IS ALSO IMMEDIATELY SENT BACK INTO AN INCARNATION. WHEN A SOUL AGREES TO AN INCARNATION IT MUST BE FULFILLED TO THE VERY END AS DETERMINED BY THEIR LIFE CHART. FATHER AND I DETERMINE WHEN THE SOUL COMES HOME.

So basically MOTHER it is viewed as the same as suicide.

YES SON, THAT IS CORRECT.

24 – *MOTHER WHAT IS THE VIEWPOINT ON BIRTH CONTROL?*

SON, IT IS ALSO NOT A GOOD THING BECAUSE THE SOUL FOR CONVENIENCE REASONS DETERMINES WHEN AN-OTHER SOUL GETS INCARNATED. FATHER AND I DETER-MINE WHEN A SOUL SHOULD BE INCARNATED NOT THE SOUL. AGAIN IT IS AN INTERFERENCE WITH THE INCAR-NATION PROCESS FOR THE ADVANCEMENT OF THE SOUL SPIRITUALITY. SOULS THEN HAVE TO WAIT TO BE INCAR-NATED TO ADVANCE THEIR 'SCHOOLING'. THIS JUST DELAYS THE COMPLETE SCHEME OF LEARNING LESSONS FOR SOUL SPIRITUALITY ADVANCEMENT. THE SOUL HAS TO WAIT FOR THE LEARNING PROCESS TO BEGIN. THE TIMING OF THE INCARNATIONS ARE ON THE SCHEDULE OF FATHER AND I, NOT THE SOUL.

25 – *MOTHER, WHAT ABOUT THE AGING PROCESS ON* EARTH *RELATED TO THESE OTHER CIVILIZATIONS IN THE UNIVERSE?*

SON, ALL INHABITANTS OF PLANETS AGE BUT *EARTH* IS THE MOST RAPID AGING PROCESS. LET ME CLARIFY. WHEN A SOUL IS IN THE INCARNATE STATE AGING IS UNIVERSAL BUT IN THE DISCARNATE STATE, THE ASTRAL BODY IS ETERNAL. *EARTH* SOULS ARE MOST RAPID IN AGING THAN OTHER CIVILIZATIONS BECAUSE THEIR SYSTEMS OF CEL-LULAR PHYSIOLOGY ARE IMMATURE IN UNDERSTAND-INGS IN COMPARISON TO THE OTHER CIVILIZATIONS.

CELLULAR UNDERSTANDINGS NEED TO BE DEVELOPED ON *EARTH* RELATED TO THE ENERGY, ATOM, MOLECULAR LEVEL.

26 – *MOTHER, IN MY RESEARCH I CAME ACROSS BERNADETTE. WHAT IS HER SIGNIFICANCE IN THE SPIRIT WORLD?*

SON, *BERNADETTE* IS A VERY HIGHLY EVOLVED SOUL WHO IS WELL RESPECTED AND LOVED IN THE CELESTIAL REALM. WE HAVE DEVELOPED A CLOSE RELATIONSHIP THROUGH THE AGES. SHE IS ONE OF THE FEW SOULS WHO RESIDES IN THE CELESTIAL REALM. SHE FIGHTS THE DARKNESS IN THE UNIVERSE BY A GREAT ENERGY OF LOVE. *BERNADETTE* KNOWS OF YOU SON AND IS ANXIOUS LIKE SO MANY OTHER HIGHLY EVOLVED SOULS TO MEET YOU. THERE ARE MANY INTRODUCTIONS I WILL TAKE YOU TO WHEN YOU RETURN HOME TO ALL OF US.

27 – *MOTHER, TELL ABOUT THE SALEM WITCH TRIALS IN 1692 IN MASSACHUSETTS AND OTHER PROSECUTIONS RELATED TO WITCHES IN THE WORLD ON THIS SIDE.*

SON, THIS WAS A TERRIBLE ACT OF INJUSTICE. THESE WOMEN AND MEN WERE PSYCHIC AND HAD SPIRITUAL ABILITIES, AS MEDIUMS TODAY. BACK THEN ANYTHING THAT WAS A SPIRITUAL OR PSYCHIC ABILITY WAS LABELED WITCHCRAFT. THE WORK OF THE DEVIL. THE DEVIL WAS DOMINANT IN PEOPLE'S LIVES. THESE PEOPLE WERE PUT TO DEATH BECAUSE THEY HAD SPECIAL PSYCHIC, SPIRITUAL ABILITIES OF CLAIRVOYANCE, CLAIRAUDIENCE, AND OTHER GIFTS.

TODAY THEY WOULD BE OUR MODERN DAY MEDIUMS. IT WAS A TRAGEDY OF MUCH PAIN AND SUFFERING FOR THESE PEOPLE AND THEIR FAMILIES. SUPERSTITION OF EVIL AND THE DEVIL RAN RAMPANT IN HISTORY WHICH WAS FUELED BY THE VARIOUS PURITANICAL RELIGIONS. THERE WAS A TOTAL LACK OF TOLERANCE OF ANYTHING THAT WAS DIFFERENT.

MOST OF THESE PEOPLE WERE WHITE ENTITIES WITH SPECIAL SPIRITUAL AND PSYCHIC ABILITIES. MANY WERE HANGED AND BURNED AT THE STAKE. THEIR SOULS WERE DAMAGED, SCARRED SO BAD BY THE TRAUMATIC DEATHS WE HAD TO PLACE THEM FOR QUITE A WHILE IN HEALING CENTERS TO RESTORE THEIR SOUL ENERGY. IT WAS A TERRIBLE MISHAP OF JUSTICE IN THE NAME OF GOD. LUNACY AND TERRIBLE ACTS OF HATRED WERE COMMITTED.

RELATED TO THE TERM WITCH, IT IS AN ANCIENT TERM TO SIGNIFY EVIL BUT MANY WERE GOOD PEOPLE, WHITE ENTITIES WITH SPIRITUAL AND PSYCHIC ABILITIES. THE IGNORANCE OF THE PEOPLE WAS GREAT.

28 – *MOTHER, TELL ME THE TRUTH ABOUT THE ASSASSINATION OF UNITED STATES PRESIDENT JOHN F. KENNEDY ON NOVEMBER 22, 1963 IN DALLAS, TEXAS.*

THE TRUTH SON, IS HE WAS A VERY GOOD SOUL, A WHITE ENTITY WHO WANTED TO BRING MORE LOVE, KINDNESS, CARING INTO THE UNITED STATES GOVERNMENT.

MANY DARK ENTITIES WERE 'WARLIKE' IN GOVERNMENT

WHO HAD NO PROBLEM IN SACRIFICING SOULS FOR THEIR PERSONAL GAIN OF MORE MONEY AND POWER. THIS COULD NOT BE TOLERATED BY MANY IN THE HIGHER POSITIONS IN THE UNITED STATES GOVERNMENT. THE CIA WORKING WITH FOREIGN GOVERNMENTS (CUBA WAS ONE OF SEVERAL FOREIGN COUNTRIES) PLOTTED HIS DEMISE. THERE WERE MANY DARK ENTITIES INVOLVED. LEE HARVEY OSWALD WAS JUST A FRONT, YOU WOULD USE THE TERM 'THE FALL GUY'. HOWEVER, THERE WERE SEVERAL SHOOTERS, CIA OPERATIVES WHO WERE IMMEDIATELY ASSASSINATED IN TURN, TO COMPLETE THE 'COVER UP'.

THIS WAS A TERRIBLE TRAGEDY IN THE ATTEMPT OF A WHITE ENTITY TO TRY AND CHANGE THINGS FOR THE BETTERMENT OF ALL SOULS IN YOUR COUNTRY AND THE WORLD. ALL THOSE DARK ENTITIES INVOLVED WERE IMMEDIATELY RECYCLED BACK INTO A FETUS UPON DEATH, NEVER TO BE ALLOWED TO GET TO THE OTHER SIDE.

As a side note, Mother and I have had many discussions about this 'recycling' of dark entity souls here on This Side because I have told Mother on This Side we are getting 'choked' by the number of dark entities now. She and Father agree something has to be done, which will be discussed when I return HOME.

CHAPTER 8

RELIGION AND TRUTH

1 – *MOTHER, WHAT IS YOUR VIEW ON RELIGION HERE ON EARTH?*

RELIGION IN ANCIENT TIMES BEFORE THE BIBLE HAD GOOD INTENTIONS ABOUT TRUTH BUT GOT TOTALLY CORRUPTED BY THE MEN WHO WANTED TO SEEK CONTROL, POWER, AND POSITION. THUS, RELIGION UNDER THE CLOAK OF TRUTH AND GOOD WAS WARPED INTO A MAN MADE INVENTION TO BENEFIT A FEW AND CONTROL THE MASSES. RELIGIONS SHOULD HAVE DEVELOPED INTO SOMETHING OF TOTAL UNCONDITIONAL LOVE BY FATHER AND I FOR ALL OUR CREATIONS. BUT INSTEAD FEAR, PUNISHMENT, THE DEVIL WERE INTRODUCED AS A MOTIVATION TO FILL PLACES OF WORSHIP. THROUGH THE NUMEROUS CENTURIES GREAT ACTS OF LUNACY AND CRUELTY WERE CREATED IN THE NAME OF GOD ON SO MANY SOULS.

2 – *MOTHER, WHY WERE YOU CAST INTO THE SHADOWS OF HISTORY ON THIS SIDE?*

SON, BECAUSE THE MALE DOMINATED RELIGIONS WOULD HAVE NEVER TOLERATED A WOMAN DEITY. IT WOULD HAVE BEEN TOO MUCH FOR THEIR MALE PRESENCE.

3 – MOTHER, AS I LEARNED ABOUT YOU AND HOW YOU WERE TREATED BY THE RELIGIONS OF THE WORLD. I DISCUSSED WITH THE COUNCIL MEMBERS ON THE OTHER SIDE AND OTHERS, I EXCLAIMED THAT TO CORRECT THIS INJUSTICE WE SHOULD HAVE A SERIES OF APPEARANCES THROUGH-OUT THE WORLD TO LET THIS SIDE KNOW ABOUT MOTHER GOD AND TO USHER IN THE AGE OF AZNA. DID YOU GIVE ME MOTHER ONE OF YOUR 'NUDGES' TO PLACE THIS IDEA IN MY MIND?

YES, I DID SON. THE TIME HAS COME FOR ME TO MAKE APPEARANCES ON YOUR SIDE. WE ARE REACHING A CRITICAL POINT IN THE HISTORY OF YOUR PLANET. THERE IS TOO MUCH EVIL THAT CONTROLS WORLD EVENTS ON YOUR SIDE. THE WHITE ENTITIES WHO CHOSE *EARTH* TO ADVANCE THEIR SPIRITUALITY MUST BE GIVEN A REASONABLE CHANCE. THUS, IT IS APPROPRIATE I MAKE A SERIES OF APPEARANCES TO GIVE HOPE TO THE WHITE ENTITIES, THE LOVING ENTITIES ON YOUR SIDE. YES, IT WAS MY IDEA I TRANSFERRED TO YOU.

4 – MOTHER, YOU TALKED ABOUT THE DARK EVIL ENTITIES OF THE UNIVERSE HOWEVER, RELATED TO THIS IS THERE A SATAN OR A DEVIL?

NO SON THERE IS NO DEVIL OR SATAN. THAT IS A FABRICATION OF RELIGIONS THROUGHOUT HISTORY ON YOUR SIDE TO USE FEAR TO CONTROL SOULS FOR THE BENEFIT OF THE RELIGION. FEAR IS A VERY POWERFUL WEAPON IN CONTROLLING SOULS.

5 – MOTHER, YOU APPEARED AT LOURDES, FATIMA, MEDJU-GORJE, GUADALUPE, WHY?

BECAUSE THEY WERE CRITICAL TIME PERIODS IN THE HISTORY OF YOUR PLANET, TO GIVE HOPE TO THE WHITE ENTITIES.

6 – MOTHER, RELIGIONS ON EARTH CREATED ALL THESE PLACES OF WORSHIP, TELL ME ABOUT THIS.

SON, THIS WAS TOTALLY UNNECESSARY BECAUSE FATHER AND I ARE EVERYWHERE. YOU CAN WORSHIP, PRAY WITH FATHER AND I ANYWHERE. THESE BUILDINGS OF WORSHIP WERE CREATED BY MEN WHO WANTED TO HAVE RECOGNITION OF THEIR STATURE IN SOCIETY. THESE BUILDINGS OF WORSHIP WERE BUILT BY MEN FOR THEIR ADVANTAGES IN THE COMMUNITY. IT WAS TOTALLY UN-NECESSARY BUT THIS ALSO IS LINKED TO THE IDEA OF CONTROL OF THE PEOPLE. THEY HAD TO ATTEND A PLACE UNDER THE TERMS OF RELIGIOUS LEADERS.

7 – MOTHER, IN CHRISTIANITY THROUGH HISTORY THERE HAVE BEEN MANY SAINTS. ARE SAINTS TREATED DIFFERENT-LY ON THE OTHER SIDE?

SON, NO THEY ARE NOT. DEPENDING ON THE VALIDITY OF THEIR ACTIONS DURING INCARNATIONS THEY ARE TREATED LIKE ALL OTHER SOULS. THERE HAVE BEEN TRUE HIGHLY EVOLVED SPIRITS BASED ON THEIR AC-TIONS IN INCARNATIONS AND OTHERS WERE FALSE. IT ALL DEPENDS ON THEIR TRUTH WITHIN THEIR HEART.

SAINT IS NOT THE PROPER WORD TO USE; JUST A SOUL WHO HAS EVOLVED TO A HIGH LEVEL OF SPIRITUALITY BY THEIR ACTIONS DURING AN INCARNATION. THERE HAVE BEEN SAINTS THAT WERE FALSE IN THEIR HEART.

8 – *MOTHER, DO OTHER PLANETS HAVE RELIGION IN THE UNIVERSE?*

NO SON, *EARTH* IS THE ONLY PLANET IN THE UNIVERSE WITH RELIGION. THE OTHER PLANETS HAVE ATTAINED THE LEVEL OF HIGH SPIRITUALITY, UNDERSTANDING THEIR RELATIONSHIP TO FATHER AND I, WHICH IS SIMPLY ETERNAL UNCONDITIONAL LOVE AND LOVE OF EACH OTHER.

9 – *MOTHER, TELL ME ABOUT MOSES AND THE TEN COMMANDMENTS AND MT. SINAI.*

SON, THIS IS ALL A 'MADE UP' STORY BY THE RELIGIOUS LEADERS AT THE TIME. MOSES DID EXIST. HE WAS A RELIGIOUS LEADER OF CONSIDERABLE WEIGHT, INFLUENCE. HOWEVER WHAT WAS TOLD ABOUT THE 10 COMMANDMENTS WAS A PLOY TO CONTROL THE ILLITERATE POPULATION WHO COULD NOT READ OR WRITE. SO THEY JUST ACCEPTED THE WORD OF THE MALE RELIGIOUS LEADERS AT THE TIME. THE 10 COMMANDMENTS WERE MADE UP BY THE RELIGIOUS LEADERS TO AGAIN CONTROL THE POPULATION TO DO WHAT THEY TOLD THE PEOPLE TO DO. IT MAKES FOR GREAT ENTERTAINMENT BUT HAD NOTHING TO DO WITH FATHER AND I.

IT IS SAD BECAUSE MANY RELIGIOUS LEADERS OF THE TIME WERE VERY CORRUPT AND ONLY SOUGHT POWER AND STATURE IN THE COMMUNITY. THE WELLBEING OF THE PEOPLE WAS NEVER CONSIDERED.

MOSES WAS A DARK ENTITY NOT GRAY OR WHITE. WHEN HE RETURNED TO OUR SIDE HE WAS IMMEDIATELY SENT BACK TO YOUR SIDE. MOSES HAS BEEN SENT BACK TO YOUR SIDE NUMEROUS TIMES AS DIFFERENT PEOPLE IN HISTORY WITH ALWAYS EVIL INTENT IN HIS INCARNA-TIONS.

AS I SAID NO DARK ENTITY IS EVER ALLOWED TO STAY ON OUR SIDE. OUR SIDE IS ONLY FOR WHITE ENTITIES AND IN THE LOWEST ASTRAL PLANES FOR THE GRAY ENTITIES TO GIVE THEM THE OPPORTUNITY TO BETTER THEM-SELVES TO THE HIGHER ASTRAL PLANES WHERE WHITE ENTITIES RESIDE.

THROUGHOUT HISTORY MANY RELIGIOUS LEADERS WERE DARK ENTITIES WHO WERE ONLY INTERESTED IN POWER AND CONTROL OF THE PEOPLE.

10 – *WHAT ABOUT WHEN MOSES PARTED THE SEA AS THE EGYPTIAN ARMY WAS CHASING THE ISRAELITES?*

AGAIN SON, IT MAKES FOR GREAT ENTERTAINMENT BUT THIS NEVER HAPPENED. IT WAS A PLOY TO STRIKE FEAR INTO THE HEART OF FUTURE GENERATIONS OF THE POWER OF GOD AND RELIGIOUS LEADERS. THAT YOU HAD BETTER LISTEN TO US, IF YOU WANT TO BE SAVED. IT

WAS ABOUT FEAR IN CONTROL OF THE PEOPLE. SO MUCH EXPLOITATION OF THE PEOPLE WAS DONE BY RELIGIOUS LEADERS FOR SEVERAL THOUSANDS OF YEARS. TODAY IN YOUR TIME IT IS STILL ONGOING OF CONTROL OF THE PEOPLE. RELIGIOUS LEADERS CONSIDER THIS AN EASY WAY TO GAIN POWER BY FEAR NOT LOVE.

11 – *MOTHER TELL ME ABOUT THE MANY CATHOLIC INQUISITIONS IN EUROPE.*

SON, IT WAS A TERRIBLE TIME PERIOD IN EUROPE OF SEVERAL CENTURIES. PEOPLE WERE FORCED TO CONVERT TO CATHOLICISM OR FACE DEATH. THERE WAS NO FREEDOM OF CHOICE. THE LAW OF FREE WILL WAS VIOLATED. HUNDREDS, THOUSANDS OF EXECUTIONS TOOK PLACE. THE PEOPLE BEING EXECUTED MANY WERE GOOD SOULS, WHITE ENTITIES. THE LEADERS OF THE CATHOLIC CHURCH WANTED MORE AND MORE POWER OVER THE PEOPLE. MANY WERE FORCED TO BECOME CATHOLIC OR FACE DEATH. MANY OF THESE LEADERS OF THE CATHOLIC CHURCH IN SEVERAL EUROPEAN COUNTRIES DURING THOSE CENTURIES WERE DARK ENTITIES, HIGHLY EVIL. A FEW GRAY BUT MOST DARK ENTITIES TO FORCE THEIR RULE ON THE PEOPLE TO GAIN MORE POWER, RICHES, AND POSITION OVER THE POPULATION IN THOSE CENTURIES.

IT WAS UNDER THE GUISE OF RELIGIOUS GOOD BUT WAS EVIL THROUGH AND THROUGH. SOME OF THESE RELIGIOUS DARK ENTITIES WERE THE WORST, MOST EVIL ONES TO EVER ENCOUNTER. IT VIOLATED THE LAW OF FREE WILL IN THE UNIVERSE WHICH IS ESSENTIAL. THIS

ANGERED FATHER AND I VERY MUCH. THE EXECUTED WHITE ENTITIES HAD TO HAVE THEIR SOULS REHABILITATED EXTENSIVELY WHEN THEY MADE THE TRANSITION HOME. IT TRULY WAS A DARK CHAPTER IN THE HISTORY OF YOUR CIVILIZATION.

12 – *MOTHER WHAT ABOUT RELIGIOUS DARK ENTITIES AND OTHER PROFESSIONS?*

I HAVE FOUND RELIGIOUS LEADERS HAVE A MUCH HIGHER NUMBER OF DARK ENTITIES THROUGH HISTORY BECAUSE OF THE EASY POWER AND CONTROL OF THE PEOPLE. OTHER PROFESSIONS HAVE DARK ENTITIES OF COURSE BUT RELIGIOUS LEADERSHIP ATTRACTS DARK ENTITIES BECAUSE OF THE HUNGER FOR POWER, STATURE, AND CONTROL OF PEOPLE AND TO SACRIFICE PEOPLE FOR THEIR OWN BENEFIT.

13 – *MOTHER WHAT WILL BE THE EVOLUTION OF RELIGION ON PLANET* EARTH *IN THE FUTURE?*

SON, RELIGION ON YOUR PLANET WILL DRAMATICALLY DECLINE AS PEOPLE LEARN MORE AND MORE ABOUT SPIRITUALISM AND YOU ARE ETERNAL. THAT THERE IS NO DEATH. GREATER STRIDES WILL BE MADE ON CONSCIOUSNESS AND UNDERSTANDING THAT CONSCIOUSNESS SURVIVES DEATH. THE RESULTS WILL BE THE DECLINE IN THE MAN MADE RELIGIONS, OBSOLESCENCE OF CEMETERIES, MORTICIANS, AND FUNERAL HOMES. CHURCHES WILL BECOME VACANT.

THIS COMPLETE IDEA OF DEATH WILL BE TOTALLY CHANGED AS NOTHING TO FEAR BUT ACTUALLY A BEGINNING IN GOING HOME. IT WILL TAKE APPROXIMATELY A HUNDRED YEARS TO TRULY TAKE HOLD AMONG THE PEOPLE ON YOUR SIDE OF *EARTH.*

14 – MOTHER, WHAT WILL BE THE EFFECT ON MEDICINE IN THAT THERE IS NO DEATH?

SON, THE VIEWPOINTS IN MEDICINE WILL DRAMATICALLY CHANGE TO AN EMPHASIS ON QUALITY OF LIFE WHILE PEOPLE ARE HERE ON THIS SIDE. HOSPICE CENTERS WILL RISE GREATLY IN HELPING TO MAKE THE TRANSITION HOME. MEDICINE WILL STILL BE VERY ACTIVE FOR QUALITY OF HEALTH AFFECTING QUALITY OF LIFE WHILE ON THIS SIDE.

CHAPTER 9

THE BIBLE AND JESUS

1 – MOTHER, TELL ME ABOUT THE BIBLE AND ITS TRUTH.

THE BIBLE WAS CREATED FROM MANY BOOKS OF FOLLOWERS OF JESUS, WHO WAS ONE OF THE MESSENGERS OF FATHER AND I. MANY BOOKS OF THE BIBLE WERE CHANGED OR DELETED BECAUSE IT DID NOT FIT THE BELIEFS OF THE ELDERS OF RELIGIONS. WORDS, SENTENCES WERE CHANGED THROUGH THE MANY CENTURIES AND TRANSLATIONS. BOOKS WERE DISCARDED ABOUT MYSELF AND REINCARNATION. THE BIBLE WAS SHAPED TO FIT THE NEEDS OF THE RELIGIOUS LEADERS TO THE POINT THAT MANY TRUTHS WERE CHANGED. THE BIBLE WAS USED AS A TOOL TO CONTROL SOULS BY THE CHURCH LEADERS. IN THE END THE BIBLE THROUGH TIME AND TRANSLATIONS HAD LITTLE RESEMBLANCE TO THE ORIGINAL SCRIPTURES. IT BECAME AN INSTRUMENT OF CONTROL OVER SOULS.

2 – MOTHER, JESUS IS CENTRAL IN THE RELIGIONS OF CHRISTIANITY, TELL ME ABOUT JESUS.

SON, JESUS IS A VERY HIGHLY EVOLVED SOUL FROM THE PLANET *NUVO*. SOME OF THE HIGHEST SOULS IN SPIRITUALITY AND LOVE COME FROM *NUVO*. BEFORE THE COMPLETION OF THE UNIVERSE SEVERAL SOULS WERE

SELECTED FOR SPECIFIC TASKS. JESUS WAS ASSIGNED THE TASK OF COMING TO *EARTH* TO TEACH AND LEAVE A LEGACY OF LOVE AND SPIRITUALITY. TEACHING ABOUT THE UNCONDITIONAL LOVE THAT FATHER AND I HAVE FOR ALL OUR CREATIONS. HOWEVER, THE LEADERS OF THE CHURCH CHANGED MANY OF THE WORDS JESUS SPOKE AND ADAPTED THEIR OWN INTERPRETATIONS TO SUIT THEIR PURPOSES OF CONTROL AND POWER.

3 – *MOTHER WAS THERE A PONTIUS PILATE AS A ROMAN OFFICIAL AND THE TRIAL THAT SENTENCED JESUS TO CRUCIFIXION?*

YES, SON PONTIUS PILATE DID EXIST AND HE WAS GOVERNOR OF THE PROVINCE. THERE ALSO WAS A TRIAL BECAUSE THE JEWISH RELIGIOUS LEADERS WANTED JESUS TO BE KILLED BECAUSE HE TALKED OF UNCONDITIONAL LOVE BY FATHER AND I AND SOULS WERE AUTOMATICALLY FORGIVEN FOR THEIR SINS.

THIS WAS TOTALLY AGAINST THE TEACHINGS OF THE JEWISH LEADERS WHO NEEDED TO CONTROL THE PEOPLE. THUS, A SYSTEM OF PUNISHMENT WAS DEVISED AS A FEAR MECHANISM OF CONTROL.

PONTIUS PILATE DID SENTENCE JESUS TO CRUCIFIXION BECAUSE OF THE PRESSURE OF THE JEWISH RELIGIOUS LEADERS. HOWEVER, THE STORY OF HIM WASHING HIS HANDS OF THE SITUATION IS NOT TRUE. HE DID CARRY OUT THE SENTENCE.

4 – MOTHER, DID JESUS DIE ON THE CROSS AND THEN RISE FROM THE DEAD?

SON, NO HE DID NOT DIE ON THE CROSS. IT MADE A CONVENIENT STORY FOR THE CHURCH LEADERS THROUGH THE CENTURIES. THAT HE DIED ON THE CROSS TO HAVE PEOPLE'S SINS FORGIVEN. FIRST, FATHER AND I LOVE ALL OUR SOULS WE CREATED UNCONDITIONALLY, NO MATTER HOW MANY SINS/MISTAKES THEY MAKE. THERE IS NO NEED FOR FORGIVENESS. THIS WAS A PLAY BY CHURCH LEADERS OF SIN/PUNISHMENT/REPENTANCE TO GAIN CONTROL AND POWER OVER THE PEOPLE.

JESUS WAS PLACED ON THE CROSS, YES, BUT WAS TAKEN DOWN SHORTLY AT NIGHT BY TWO ROMAN SOLDIERS, FRIENDS OF THE FAMILY, AND PLACED ON A SHIP TO FRANCE, WHERE HE AND HIS WIFE MARY MAGDALENE HAD A FAMILY OF SEVERAL CHILDREN. AFTER, JESUS TRAVELED EXTENSIVELY THROUGHOUT THE MIDDLE EAST AND ASIA TO STUDY THE VARIOUS FORMS OF FAITH AND RELIGIONS. IT WAS A CONVENIENT STORY TO HAVE HIM DIE ON THE CROSS FOR OUR SINS AND RISE FROM THE DEAD TO FIT THE POWER HUNGRY NEEDS OF FUTURE CHURCH LEADERS.

5 – MOTHER, SO WHAT ABOUT THE STORIES OF THE LAST SUPPER, JUDAS, THE SPEAR IN THE SIDE OF JESUS WHILE ON THE CROSS, THE HOLY SPIRIT VISITING THE APOSTLES LATER AS THEY WERE HIDING?

SON THIS WAS ALL FABRICATION. WITH TIME ALL THESE

STORIES SLOWLY EVOLVED. THEY WERE STORIES THAT IS ALL TO FIT THE NEEDS OF CHURCH LEADERS. IN THOSE TIMES MOST OF THE PEOPLE WERE ILLITERATE, COULD NOT READ OR WRITE, SO THEY ACCEPTED WHAT THE EDUCATED CHURCH LEADERS TOLD THEM.

THE DECEIT AND LIES OF THE CHURCH LEADERS FOR THEIR OWN GAIN HAS BOTHERED FATHER AND I. SEVERAL CHURCH LEADERS IN HISTORY ARE DARK AND GRAY ENTITIES. THROUGH THE CENTURIES THERE WAS MUCH EVIL WITHIN RELIGIONS AND AMONGST THEIR LEADERS. THESE RELIGIOUS DARK ENTITIES NEVER GET TO THE OTHER SIDE. THEY JUST HAVE THEIR SOULS RECYCLED ON YOUR SIDE AND THE GRAY ENTITIES FIND THEMSELVES IN THE LOWEST ASTRAL LEVELS TO BE GIVEN THE OPPORTUNITY TO ADVANCE THEIR SPIRITUALITY. HOWEVER, MANY ACTUALLY TURN TO BECOME DARK ENTITIES.

6 – MOTHER, TELL ME ABOUT THE FAMOUS STORY THAT JESUS ROSE LAZARUS FROM THE DEAD.

SON, THIS ALSO WAS FABRICATION WITH A TWIST. LAZARUS WAS INDEED DEAD FROM ILLNESS AND JESUS ARRIVED TOO LATE TO HELP. JESUS DID ATTEMPT TO RISE LAZARUS FROM THE DEAD TO NO AVAIL. HOWEVER, THE LOCAL PEOPLE DECIDED TO TELL THE STORY OTHERWISE THAT JESUS WAS SUCCESSFUL. YES, THERE WAS A LAZARUS AND JESUS DID ATTEMPT TO CALL OUT AND RISE HIM FROM THE DEAD BUT IT WAS NOT SUCCESSFUL. REMEMBER THE PEOPLE WERE HIGHLY ILLITERATE, SUSCEPTIBLE TO SUPERSTITION AND AS TIME PASSED THE STORY MORPHED INTO A GREAT SUCCESS FOR JESUS

RAISING LAZARUS FROM THE DEAD. THE PEOPLE WANT-
ED TO SEE JESUS BEING SUCCESSFUL.

7 – *MOTHER, YOU SAID JESUS CAME FROM THE PLANET*
NUVO, *TELL ME ABOUT THIS.*

JESUS CAME FROM *NUVO*. WHITE ENTITY SOULS FROM
OTHER PARTS OF THE UNIVERSE CAN VISIT *NUVO*, BUT
CANNOT STAY. IT IS ONE OF THE PLACES IN THE UNIVERSE
OF THE HIGHEST SPIRITUALITY. IT IS A WONDERFUL
PLANET OF BEAUTY, TRANQUILITY, MEDITATION, LOVE,
AND SERVICE TO ALL. THERE IS A HIERARCHY ON *NUVO*
OF LEADERSHIP. BECAUSE OF THE UNIVERSE MATRIX
OF CONSCIOUSNESS THEY KNOW OF YOU SON, WHAT
YOU HAVE ACHIEVED, ARE ACHIEVING AT PRESENT, AND
YOUR TASKS AHEAD. THEY KNOW YOU ARE THE SON OF
FATHER AND I BUT HOLD YOU IN HIGH ESTEEM FOR
YOUR ACHIEVEMENTS.

CHAPTER 10

REINCARNATION

1 – MOTHER, TELL ME ABOUT HOW REINCARNATION CAME ABOUT.

SON, FATHER AND I WANTED A WAY TO EDUCATE OUR SOULS IN THE UNIVERSE. THE BEST WAY TO DO THIS WAS TO LEARN VARIOUS LESSONS OF SPIRITUALITY FOR THE SOUL IN ACTUAL LIFE. THIS WOULD NEVER BE ACHIEVED IN ONE LIFE. THUS, A SOUL HAD TO HAVE MULTIPLE LIVES TO PROGRESS TO HIGHER STATES OF SPIRITUALITY. THIS REINCARNATION SCHEME IS A LONG PROCESS BUT MUCH SHORTER THAN A SOUL THAT NEVER EXPERIENCES REINCARNATION. THERE ARE MANY SOULS IN THE UNIVERSE THAT WILL NEVER REINCARNATE. THEIR SPIRITUAL JOURNEY IS MUCH LONGER. LIVING A LIFE IS LEARNING.

2 – MOTHER, DO ALL SOULS IN THE UNIVERSE ON ALL THE OTHER SIDES OF PLANETS HAVE THE OPPORTUNITY TO REINCARNATE ON ALL PLANETS?

YES SON, THEY DO. THIS IS A UNIVERSAL OPPORTUNITY. AS I SAID MANY SOULS DO NOT TAKE ADVANTAGE OF THIS REINCARNATION OPPORTUNITY. THE MOST HIGHLY EVOLVED SOULS ARE THE ONES WHO REINCARNATE TO VARIOUS DEGREES. YOU SON, HAVE BECOME A HIGHLY EVOLVED SOUL BY ALL YOUR PAST LIVES THROUGH

REINCARNATION. FATHER AND I ARE SO PROUD OF YOU. YOU HAVE TURNED OUT EVEN BETTER THAN WE ANTICIPATED.

3 – MOTHER, I HAVE HAD 62 INCARNATIONS, WHERE HAVE THEY BEEN SPENT IN THE UNIVERSE?

ALMOST ALL OF YOUR INCARNATIONS HAVE BEEN SPENT ON *EARTH*. A FEW HAVE BEEN SPENT ON OTHER WORLDS. THAT IS WHY YOU HAVE ADVANCED SO RAPIDLY IN YOUR SPIRITUALITY. FATHER AND I ARE VERY PROUD OF YOU. WE ARE SO ANXIOUS TO TAKE YOU HOME FOR ETERNITY. SON, WE LOVE YOU VERY MUCH.

4 – MOTHER, YOU MENTIONED THAT MANY HIGHLY EVOLVED SOULS REINCARNATE ON EARTH, WHY IS THIS SO?

BECAUSE SON, THEY TAKE ON THE GREAT CHALLENGES ON *EARTH* TO ADVANCE THEIR SOUL SPIRITUALITY TO MUCH HIGHER LEVELS. THESE SOULS WILL EXPERIENCE EVERYTHING HERE ON ALL LEVELS OF CONSCIOUSNESS. THESE HIGHLY EVOLVED SOULS WILL ADVANCE FASTER IN THE DEVELOPMENT OF THEIR SPIRITUALITY.

THERE ARE MANY SOULS IN THE UNIVERSE THAT WILL NOT COME TO *EARTH* BECAUSE OF FEAR OF THE GREAT CHALLENGES.

5 – MOTHER, IT HAS BEEN STATED THAT SOULS CAN HAVE BE-TWEEN 700 TO 1,000 INCARNATIONS OR PAST LIVES. MOTHER I ONLY HAD 62 INCLUDING THIS ONE, WHY?

SON, MOST SOULS ARE NOT AS EVOLVED AS YOU WERE FROM THE BEGINNING. YES, SOULS CAN HAVE BETWEEN 700 TO 1,000 INCARNATIONS. HOWEVER, YOU ONLY RE-QUIRED 62. SON, I HAVE BEEN TRYING TO TELL YOU. YOU ARE A VERY EXCEPTIONAL SOUL. MOST SOULS HAVE A LONGER LEARNING PROCESS TO ADVANCE. YOU AD-VANCED SO QUICKLY BECAUSE YOU ARE VERY PERCEPTIVE AND HAVE A HIGHER DEGREE OF INTELLIGENCE. SON, YOU DID NOT NEED ALL THE PAST LIVES TO ADVANCE.

6 – *MOTHER, DO SOULS INCARNATE WITH LIVES AT THE SAME TIME?*

YES SON, THEY DO, IT IS NOT AS OFTEN AS PEOPLE THINK BUT IT OCCURS. THE REASONS BEING THE SOUL WANTS TO ACCELERATE THEIR LEARNING PROCESS. MOST SOULS DON'T DO LIVES AT THE SAME TIME. SON, YOU NEVER HAD TO DO PAST LIVES SIMULTANEOUSLY BECAUSE YOU WERE ADVANCING SO RAPIDLY ON YOUR OWN WITH SINGLE INCARNATIONS.

CHAPTER 11

THE OTHER SIDE OF *EARTH*

1 – MOTHER, COULD YOU DESCRIBE FOR ME THE OTHER SIDE OF PLANET EARTH?

SON, IT IS A BEAUTIFUL VERSION OF YOUR SIDE. IT IS PRISTINE, LESS WATER, MORE LAND MASS. EVERYTHING IS ETERNAL AND NEVER DECAYS. IT HAS ALL THE PLACES OF YOUR SIDE PLUS ATLANTIS AND LEMURIA CONTINENTS. ALL FORMS OF LIFE ARE LOVING AND FRIENDLY. ALL THE RECORDS OF CIVILIZATIONS OF *EARTH* FROM THE EARLIEST ARE AVAILABLE IN BRAND NEW CONDITION.

MANY SOULS EXPLORE *EARTH* FROM OUR SIDE WITHOUT THE DISADVANTAGES OF TRAVEL, EXPENSE, POLLUTION, CROWDS. WE JUST THINK IT AND YOU ARE THERE. IT IS A WONDERFUL RESOURCE FOR EXPLORING AND EDUCATION. PLUS, THERE ARE ALWAYS OUR VAST LIBRARIES AND HALL OF RECORDS. ANY EXPERIENCE OR EVENT IN HUMAN HISTORY CAN BE LIVED AGAIN BY MERGING ONE'S ENERGY INTO THE EVENT. FATHER AND I WANTED EASY ACCESS TO KNOWLEDGE.

2 – MOTHER, DO OTHER PLANETS HAVE THE OTHER SIDE AND WHAT ARE THEIR LIFE FORMS?

SON, ALL INHABITED PLANETS HAVE THE OTHER SIDE.

THEY ARE ALL SPIRIT BEINGS TAKING ON A HUMAN FORM WITH VARIANCES AS FATHER AND I DO.

3 – *MOTHER, DID HUMAN LIFE ORIGINATE ON EARTH?*

NO SON, HUMAN LIFE AS YOU KNOW IT CAME FROM SEVERAL OTHER PLANETS. OTHER PLANETS IN YOUR SOLAR SYSTEM HAD HUMAN LIFE AT ONE TIME.

4 – *MOTHER, TELL ME ABOUT THE CHARACTERISTICS OF THE MENTAL OR CAUSAL REALM.*

SON, THIS DIMENSION IS JUST ABOVE THE HIGHEST ASTRAL PLANE. IT IS WHERE YOUR BODY EXISTENCE BECOMES LIGHTER, MORE SPIRITUAL, LESS DENSE. YOU DO NOT TRAVEL BY WALKING BUT JUST FLY OR FLOAT IN THE RAREFIED ATMOSPHERE.

EVERYTHING IS A MUCH HIGHER DEGREE OF CONSCIOUSNESS. THE SPIRITUAL LEVEL IS THE HIGHEST. BEFORE ONE GETS TO THE CELESTIAL REALM, WHICH IS THE HIGHEST DIMENSION IN THE UNIVERSE OF SPIRITUALITY. MOSTLY THE MENTAL OR CAUSAL REALM IS OCCUPIED BY THE SELECT HIGHEST EVOLVED ENTITIES, SOMETIMES THEY HAVE BEEN CALLED THE MASTERS. THEIR KNOWLEDGE OF THE UNIVERSE IS GREAT. THIS REALM IS VERY BEAUTIFUL WITH ENDLESS GARDENS AND BODIES OF WATER. THERE ARE NO CITIES IN THIS REALM. IT IS CALLED THE MENTAL OR CAUSAL REALM BECAUSE IT IS AT ONE OF THE HIGHEST LEVELS OF CONSCIOUSNESS AND THE POWER OF THOUGHT. IT IS A VERY LOVING REALM WHERE THE SELECT SPIRITS DO EVERYTHING OUT OF LOVE AND

CHAPTER 11

SERVICE FOR EACH OTHER. FATHER AND I ARE VERY PROUD OF THIS REALM BECAUSE OF THE LEVEL OF LOVE. ALL THE OTHER PLANETS THAT ARE INHABITED HAVE A MENTAL OR CAUSAL REALM ON THEIR OTHER SIDE.

As a side note, Mother tells me we will go visit the Mental or Causal realms. There is so much she wants to show me with numerous discussions with Father and her.

5 – *MOTHER, TELL ME ABOUT THE CELESTIAL REALM.*

SON, IT IS THE HIGHEST DIMENSION OR REALM IN THE UNIVERSE. ALL THE INHABITED PLANETS HAVE THEIR CELESTIAL REALM AND ALL THE OTHER LEVELS I DESCRIBED. THE CELESTIAL REALM IS WHERE FATHER AND I RESIDE, WITH THE ANGELS AND THE PRESENCE. THE PRESENCE IS A COMBINATION OF HIGHLY EVOLVED SPIRITS. THEY ARE TOTALLY IN SPIRIT FORM BY THEIR CHOICE. THE CELESTIAL REALM IS INCREDIBLY BEAUTIFUL. THE COLORS, THE ATMOSPHERE IS ONE OF SHEER BEAUTY. NO SOULS RESIDE THERE EXCEPT FATHER AND I AND THE ANGELS. IT IS THE HIGHEST LEVEL OF SPIRITUALITY IN THE UNIVERSE. THERE ARE NO CLOUDS OR MIST, VERY CLEAR WITH INCREDIBLE BEAUTY OF COLORS AND LANDSCAPES. I WILL TAKE YOU THERE MY SON TO SEE FOR YOURSELF.

6 – *MOTHER, ARE THERE LEVELS OR DIMENSIONS BELOW THE LOWEST ASTRAL LEVEL?*

YES SON, THERE ARE. THESE WE CALL THE UNDERWORLD. THERE ARE SEVERAL LEVELS THEY HAVE ALL KINDS OF SPIRITS, THOUGHTS, BEINGS THAT ARE CONTAINED IN

THESE LOWER LEVELS. SOME HAVE EVIL THOUGHTS AND BEINGS. MY FRIEND *LILITH* CONTROLS THESE LOWER WORLDS. TO MAKE SURE THEY NEVER REACH OUT TO THE HIGHER LEVELS WHERE SOULS RESIDE. IT IS LIKE A 'DUMPING GROUND' WHERE ALL EVIL THOUGHTS AND BEINGS ARE KEPT. FATHER AND I KEEP THEM BECAUSE THEY ARE STILL ALL OUR CREATIONS. WHEN YOU COME HOME SON TO US WE WILL DISCUSS THE FUTURE OF THEIR EXISTENCE.

7 – *MOTHER, TELL ME ABOUT THE SPIRITUAL CITIES ABOVE* EARTH *AS SONIA RINALDI TALKS ABOUT IN HER BOOK* ALPHA I MISSION.

SON, THERE ARE SPIRITUAL CITIES ABOVE ALL THE INHABITED PLANETS OF THE UNIVERSE. THESE SPIRITUAL CITIES ARE STATIONS ABOVE A PLANET IN THE 4TH DIMENSION TO ENHANCE SPIRITUALITY AMONG THE INHABITANTS BY AFFECTING CONSCIOUSNESS OF THAT SPECIFIC PLANET. THERE ARE TWO SPIRITUAL CITIES OVER *EARTH*, ONE OVER BRAZIL AND ONE OVER EUROPE. THESE SPIRITUAL CITIES CANNOT BE DETECTED BY YOUR PRIMITIVE TECHNOLOGIES BECAUSE THEY ARE IN THE 4TH DIMENSION. THERE HAS TO BE GREAT ADVANCEMENT IN CONSCIOUSNESS FOR *EARTH* TO DETECT AND LEARN FROM THESE SPIRITUAL CITIES. THESE SPIRITUAL CITIES HAVE CONTROLLED NUMEROUS EVENTS IN CIVILIZATION ON YOUR SIDE. HIGHLY EVOLVED SOULS LIVE IN THESE CITIES. THE FIRST SPIRITUAL CITY OVER BRAZIL IS CALLED ALPHA AND THE SECOND ONE OVER EUROPE IS CALLED BETA, IT IS OVER ROMANIA AND HUNGARY.

CHAPTER 12

TRAVEL IN THE UNIVERSE

1 – MOTHER, TELL ME ABOUT HOW IS TRAVEL POSSIBLE ACROSS DIMENSIONS. WE ARE IN THE THIRD DIMENSION, CORRECT?

YES SON, YOU ARE CORRECT, YOU ARE IN THE THIRD DIMENSION. THERE ARE NUMEROUS DIMENSIONS AND REALITIES IN THE UNIVERSE. TRAVEL IS DONE BY ADJUSTING CONSCIOUSNESS. WHAT I MEAN IS YOU REACH THESE OTHER DIMENSIONS BY THE MANIPULATION, CHANGING OF CONSCIOUSNESS. YOU CHANGE YOUR ENERGY VIBRATION FREQUENCIES BY THE POWER OF CONSCIOUSNESS. THE ENERGY OF CONSCIOUSNESS CAN CONTROL YOUR ENERGY VIBRATION FREQUENCIES. CONSCIOUSNESS IS AN ENERGY FORCE THAT CAN DETERMINE WHAT DIMENSION OR REALITY YOU WANT TO BE IN.

OUR BROTHERS AND SISTERS OF THE UNIVERSE VISIT *EARTH* ACROSS VAST DISTANCES IN THE UNIVERSE.

2 – MOTHER, HOW DO THEY DO THIS?

THEY HAVE LEARNED THE ENERGY POWER OF CONSCIOUSNESS CAN TRANSFORM MATTER OF THE SPACECRAFT, TO PLACE THE SPACECRAFT AT ANY LOCATION IN THE UNIVERSE. ON THE OTHER SIDE YOU THINK OF A LOCATION AND YOU ARE THERE. THE PRINCIPLE IS

SIMILAR TO SPACE TRAVEL IN THE UNIVERSE. ONE THINKS OF A LOCATION IN THE UNIVERSE AND YOU COUPLE THE MATTER OF THE SPACECRAFT WITH THINKING OF A UNIVERSE LOCATION AND YOU ARE THERE.

THESE ADVANCED CIVILIZATIONS HAVE LEARNED HOW TO CONTROL, MANIFEST, AND MANIPULATE THE POWER OF CONSCIOUSNESS TO TRAVEL ANYWHERE IN THE UNIVERSE. BASICALLY, IT IS TRAVEL IN THE UNIVERSE BY CONSCIOUSNESS. *EARTH* HERE IS CONSIDERED A VERY PRIMITIVE CIVILIZATION, THOUSANDS OF YEARS IN *EARTH* TIME BEHIND THESE OTHER CIVILIZATIONS.

3 – *SO MOTHER CONSCIOUSNESS IS EVERYWHERE THROUGH EVERYTHING IN THE UNIVERSE. YOU TRAVEL THROUGH THIS CONTINUUM OF CONSCIOUSNESS BY MATCHING THE VIBRATION FREQUENCIES OF THE SPACECRAFT AND EVERYTHING WITH IT, TO A LOCATION IN THE UNIVERSE BY THE POWER OF CONSCIOUSNESS.*

YES SON, THAT IS BASICALLY IT.

4 – *MOTHER, TELL ME ABOUT THE PHENOMENON OF CROP CIRCLES.*

THEY REPRESENT VISITS FROM OTHER GALAXIES AND PLANETS. IT IS THE ENERGY MARKS LEFT BEHIND OF THEIR CRAFT. THE AUTHENTIC ONES HAVE SIGNATURE SYMMETRY AS TO WHERE IN THE UNIVERSE THEY CAME FROM. THE ENERGY SHAPES THE GRASS IN A SPECIFIC WAY. THEY TRAVEL THROUGH DIMENSIONS TO VISIT *EARTH*. MANY VISITS ARE FROM *ANDROMEDA* GALAXY. SOME OF

THE SOULS THERE WERE USED TO COLONIZE *EARTH*. THE SOULS FROM *ANDROMEDA* HAVE A HIGH SPIRITUALITY AND LOVE. THEY ARE QUITE CONCERNED ABOUT WHAT IS HAPPENING TO *EARTH*.

5 – *MOTHER, TELL ME ABOUT THE BERMUDA TRIANGLE.*

SON, THE BERMUDA TRIANGLE AND OTHER SITES IN JAVA, NEBRASKA, AND A FEW OTHERS ARE DOORS BETWEEN DIMENSIONS. IT IS QUICK, EASY TRAVEL AMONG DIMENSIONS. THESE ARE LIKE ENERGY 'SHORTCUTS' TO OTHER REALMS. FATHER AND I PLACED THEM ON PLANETS FOR RAPID TRANSPORT BY INDIVIDUALS OR SPACECRAFT TO OTHER WORLDS. HOWEVER, YOU HAVE TO KNOW HOW TO USE THEM. THE ADVANCED CIVILIZATIONS USE THEM AS RAPID TRANSPORT SYSTEMS BETWEEN PLANETS. IT HAS TO DO WITH SEVERAL DIFFERENT ENERGIES OF CONSCIOUSNESS THAT LINK MANY PARTS OF THE UNIVERSE.

So Mother they are like energy consciousness 'shortcuts' to various parts of the Universe, like spacecraft one has to know how to control and manipulate your consciousness. Thus, Mother in summary consciousness is the communication and transportation system of the Universe and you have to know how to use it. That is why it is mandatory that consciousness has to be pure.

6 – *MOTHER, ARE THESE* WORMHOLES? *I WAS JUST WATCHING THE MOVIE INTERSTELLAR, AND THEY WERE TALKING ABOUT* WORMHOLES.

YES SON, THEY HAVE BEEN CALLED *WORMHOLES*. AS EXPLAINED THESE ARE SIMPLY 'SHORTCUTS' IN CONSCIOUS-

NESS THROUGHOUT THE UNIVERSE. THE ADVANCED CIVILIZATIONS KNOW HOW TO TAKE FULL ADVANTAGE OF THEM. THE *WORMHOLES* FATHER AND I HAVE PLACED THROUGHOUT THE UNIVERSE TO MAKE TRAVEL IN THE UNIVERSE CONVENIENT AND RAPID.

It is interesting. I was watching this movie *Interstellar* with Klea and it just occurred to me that what Mother was talking to me about the Bermuda Triangle and other sites were really *wormholes*. Mother just confirmed it for me as I was watching the movie.

7 – MOTHER, TELL ME ABOUT THE PHENOMENON CALLED GRAVITY WHICH HAS ELUDED UNDERSTANDING WITH OUR PRIMITIVE CIVILIZATION.

SON, GRAVITY IS A FORCE OF CONSCIOUSNESS. THERE ARE MANY FORCES OF CONSCIOUSNESS WHICH ARE NOT UNDERSTOOD BY YOUR SOULS ON *EARTH*. THE KEY IS THE UNDERSTANDING OF CONSCIOUSNESS. ITS POWERS AND HOW IT CAN BE USED. GRAVITY IS ONE OF THE MANY POWERS OF CONSCIOUSNESS THAT HOLDS EVERYTHING IN PLACE, AS FATHER HOLDS THE INTEGRITY OF THE UNIVERSE STABLE AND IN PLACE. WITHOUT GRAVITY AND FATHER'S ENORMOUS POWER TO MAINTAIN STABIL-ITY THE UNIVERSE WOULD CEASE TO EXIST. GRAVITY IS A POWER FROM CONSCIOUSNESS FOR ALL MOVING BOD-IES IN THE UNIVERSE OF ALL SIZES. IT ALSO MAINTAINS STABILITY.

CHAPTER 13

GHOSTS IN THE UNIVERSE

1 – *MOTHER, WHAT ARE GHOSTS?*

SON, GHOSTS ARE SOULS WHO HAVE GOTTEN 'CAUGHT' IN YOUR REALM, THE *EARTH* REALM, FOR MANY REASONS: EITHER A DEATH BY TRAUMATIC EVENTS, LIKE A KILL-ING, A VIOLENT DEATH, LIKE AN ACCIDENT. AN EVENT THAT HAS LEAD TO GREAT HARDSHIP. THE SOUL IS LEFT WITH GREAT EMOTION, SO IT STAYS CLOSE TO THE SITE WHERE THE DEATH TOOK PLACE. MOST SOULS GO TO THE ASTRAL PLANES BUT SOME STAY WHERE THE DEATH OCCURRED. IT IS HIGHLY EMOTIONAL WITH GREAT NEG-ATIVE EFFECTS. OVER TIME THEY ARE TAKEN HOME BY SPECIAL SPIRITS WHO DO JUST THIS ON THE OTHER SIDE TO TAKE TRAUMATIZED SOULS HOME TO THE ASTRAL PLANES.

2 – *MOTHER, HOW LONG DO TRAUMATIZED SOULS STAY 'STUCK' CLOSE TO* EARTH?

SON, IT VARIES, IT COULD BE A FEW YEARS TO HUNDREDS OF YEARS. IT DEPENDS ON THE SOUL THAT IS CAUGHT IN YOUR *EARTH* REALM.

3 – *MOTHER, CAN GHOSTS BE DARK, GRAY, OR WHITE ENTI-TIES?*

SON, THEY CAN BE ALL THREE. THE TRAUMATIC EXPERI-ENCE THAT MADE THEM GHOSTS CAN HAPPEN TO ALL THREE TYPES OF ENTITIES.

4 – *MOTHER, ARE THERE EVIL GHOSTS?*

OF COURSE SON, IF A DARK ENTITY OR GRAY HAS A TRAU-MATIC EXPERIENCE AND GETS 'CAUGHT' IN THE *EARTH'S* PHYSICAL PLANE, THEY ARE STILL EVIL. THEY WERE EVIL ON THE PHYSICAL SIDE SO THAT IS SIMPLY TRANSFERRED OVER TO THE OTHER SIDE WHICH IS CLOSEST TO *EARTH*. MANY STORIES HAVE EVOLVED ABOUT DARK ENTITY GHOSTS THROUGH HISTORY.

5 – *MOTHER, DO OTHER PLANETS IN THE UNIVERSE HAVE GHOSTS?*

NO SON, THEY DO NOT BECAUSE THE COMMUNICATION WITH THEIR OTHER SIDE IS CONSTANT. IF THERE IS A SOUL WHO IS 'STUCK' ON THE PHYSICAL SIDE OF THE PLANET THEY ARE IMMEDIATELY TAKEN TO THE OTHER SIDE. PLUS, THE OTHER PLANETS ARE A MUCH MORE LOVING, CARING ENVIRONMENT THAN *EARTH*. VIOLENCE AND HATE IS PRACTICALLY NON-EXISTENT.

6 – *MOTHER, HOW DO OTHER PLANETS COMMUNICATE WITH THEIR OTHER SIDES?*

SON, THEY COMMUNICATE BY TELEPATHY ALL THE TIME. THEY HAVE LEARNED THE POWERS OF CONSCIOUSNESS AND MIND CONTROL TO COMMUNICATE WITH THEIR

OTHER SIDES. IT IS CONSTANT AND AN 'EVERYDAY' OC-CURRENCE FOR THEM. IT IS NATURAL TO TALK TO THEIR OTHER SIDES. IT GIVES THE PEOPLE ON THE PHYSICAL SIDE GREAT COMFORT AND A GREAT SENSE OF LOVE.

7 – MOTHER, HOW DO THE PEOPLE ON OTHER PLANETS GO HOME, TO THEIR OTHER SIDE?

SON, THEY GO HOME VERY EASILY WITH NO PAIN, NO TRAUMA. SIMPLY A CLOUD IS FORMED AT THE APPROPRI-ATE TIME AND THEY JUST WALK THROUGH THE CLOUD LEAVING BEHIND THEIR TEMPORARY BODY BEHIND. IT IS QUICK AND PAINLESS. AFTER THEY HAVE LEARNED THEIR LESSONS IT IS THEN TIME TO GO HOME. THAT IS ALL.

CHAPTER 14

OTHER PLANETS OF THE UNIVERSE

1 – *MOTHER, WHAT ARE THE OTHER PLANETS OF THE UNIVERSE LIKE?*

A – THERE ARE SO MANY INHABITED PLANETS, BUT I WILL MENTION A FEW.

FIRST THERE IS *CLOUDIA*. IT IS A VERY BEAUTIFUL PLANET IN THE *ANDROMEDA* GALAXY. THE SOULS THERE HAVE EVOLVED TO A VERY HIGH LEVEL OF SPIRITUALITY. THEIR TECHNOLOGIES ARE BEYOND *EARTH'S* COMPREHENSION. FATHER AND I ARE VERY PROUD OF THIS CIVILIZATION AND HOW IT EVOLVED AND ADVANCED. THEY TRAVEL THROUGHOUT THE GALAXIES AND UNIVERSE HELPING OTHER CIVILIZATIONS. THE INHABITANTS OF *CLOUDIA* HAVE HELPED AND SAVED MANY SOULS OF THE UNIVERSE IN DIRECTING THEM TOWARDS THE LIGHT.

THE CHARACTERISTICS OF THE PLANET *CLOUDIA*, IT IS A VERY LARGE PLANET WITH MORE THAN 10 BILLION SOULS. IT HAS VAST OCEANS AND LAND MASS. IT IS A POLLUTION FREE PLANET OF PLENTY OF SUN. ALL THE SOULS ON *CLOUDIA* DO EVERYTHING TO SERVE EACH OTHER. THERE ARE NO DARK OR GRAY ENTITIES ON *CLOUDIA*. THERE LIFESPAN IS MANY HUNDREDS OF *EARTH* YEARS. THEY ARE ALL HUMAN, SIMILAR TO HUMANS ON *EARTH*.

THE INHABITANTS OF *CLOUDIA* HAVE VISITED *EARTH* MANY TIMES AND ARE QUITE WORRIED ABOUT THE DIRECTION *EARTH* IS GOING IN.

I WILL TAKE YOU THERE. THEY KNOW OF YOUR ACHIEVEMENTS THROUGH THE MATRIX OF CONSCIOUSNESS AND THE LEADERS, AS SO MANY, ARE ANXIOUS TO MEET YOU, MY SON.

B – *XENA* (THE X IS PRONOUNCED LIKE THE LETTER Z)

MOTHER, TELL ME ABOUT THE PLANET XENA.

IT IS ALSO A VERY BEAUTIFUL PLANET IN THE GALAXY OF THE *CRAB NEBULA*. IT IS MUCH FURTHER AWAY FROM *EARTH* THAN *CLOUDIA* IN THE *ANDROMEDA* GALAXY. IT IS ALSO A VERY LARGE PLANET WITH TWO SUNS. THE SUNS ARE SMALL IN COMPARISON TO OTHER SUNS. THERE ARE ABOUT 6 BILLION SOULS ON *XENA*. THEY ARE ALSO HUMAN LIKE IN APPEARANCE AS THE INHABITANTS OF *EARTH*. A HIGHLY SPIRITUAL PEOPLE WHO HAVE TRAVELED TO *EARTH* MANY TIMES. THEIR CONCERN FOR *EARTH* IS GREAT. THE WARLIKE NATURE AND VIOLENCE ON *EARTH* IS QUITE DISTURBING TO THEM. THEIR WORLD IS MOSTLY LAND MASS WITH SMALL OCEANS. IT IS STILL A VERY BEAUTIFUL PLANET AND THE COLORS EXHIBITED ARE VERY ATTRACTIVE BECAUSE OF THE TWO SUNS. THERE ARE SEVERAL MOONS AROUND *XENA*. THE LIFESPAN OF THE PEOPLE IS ALSO SEVERAL HUNDRED *EARTH* YEARS. IT IS UNIQUE BECAUSE OF THE TWO SUNS AND SEVERAL MOONS. IT IS ONE OF MY FAVORITE PLACES TO VISIT. THE PEOPLE ARE SO LOVING AND WONDER-

FUL. HERE ALSO THERE ARE NO DARK ENTITIES IN THIS UNIQUE AND BEAUTIFUL PLANET. BOTH PLANETS *CLOUD-IA* AND *XENA* IN THEIR VERY LONG HISTORIES DID HAVE WARS BUT NOT LIKE *EARTH*. *EARTH* BY FAR IS THE MOST VIOLENT, WARLIKE PLANET IN THE UNIVERSE BECAUSE OF THE PRESENCE OF SO MANY DARK AND GRAY ENTITIES.

C – *HPYZA* (PRONOUNCED HYPE ZA)

MOTHER, TELL ME ABOUT THE PLANET HPYZA.

SON, THE PLANET *HPYZA* IS ALSO VERY BEAUTIFUL WITH SEVEN RINGS AROUND IT WITH ALL KINDS OF COLORS. IT IS ALSO QUITE LARGE IN COMPARISON TO OTHER PLAN-ETS. IT IS IN THE GALAXY *ARIEN* WHICH IS ALSO VERY FAR IN DISTANCE FROM *EARTH*. THIS GALAXY IS CALLED BY OTHER NAMES. IT HAS ONE SUN IN ITS SOLAR SYSTEM. THE PEOPLE, WHICH ARE ALSO HUMAN LIKE, LIVE ON THE RINGS AND THE PLANET SURFACE. THE SOULS THAT LIVE ON THE RINGS LIVE IN DOMES THAT ARE LIGHTER THAN THE MASS OF THE RINGS. SO WITH THEIR HIGH-LY ADVANCED TECHNOLOGY THEY CAN ACTUALLY FLOAT ON THE RINGS. THE PLANET SURFACE HAS LARGE OCEANS AND NUMEROUS CONTINENTS.

THE LEVEL OF SPIRITUALITY IS ALSO VERY EVOLVED BY THE PEOPLE ON THIS PLANET WITH NO DARK OR GRAY ENTITIES, JUST WHITE ENTITIES. *HPYZA* HAD A TUR-BULENT HISTORY BUT NOTHING LIKE *EARTH*. THERE IS NO PLANET IN THE UNIVERSE WITH THE EVIL THAT *EARTH* HAS MANIFESTED THROUGH THE THOUSANDS OF YEARS BECAUSE OF THE MULTITUDE OF DARK AND GRAY

ENTITIES. THEY HAVE VISITED *EARTH* ALSO AND ARE CONCERNED AT THE LEVEL OF EVIL AND CRUELTY.

THE PEOPLE'S LIFESPAN IS OVER A THOUSAND *EARTH* YEARS. THEY, LIKE THE OTHER PLANETS MENTIONED, HAVE SHARED THEIR ADVANCED TECHNOLOGIES WITH NUMEROUS CIVILIZATIONS IN THE UNIVERSE. THERE ARE 9-10 BILLION SOULS LIVING ON *HPYZA*.

D – *ACRONY*

MOTHER, TELL ME ABOUT THE PLANET ACRONY.

ACRONY SON, IS LIKE THE OTHERS A BEAUTIFUL PLANET AND QUITE UNIQUE. *ACRONY* IS IN THE GALAXY *ORIEN*. IT HAS TWO SUNS ALSO AS *XENA* BUT THE SUNS ARE MUCH LARGER AND *ACRONY* IS A SMALL PLANET WITH VAST OCEANS AND SMALL LAND MASS. MANY OF THE SOULS LIVE IN THE OCEANS IN DOMED CITIES AT THE BOTTOM OF THE OCEANS AT VARIOUS LOCATIONS. ON THE SURFACE OF THE PLANET THERE IS NO REQUIRE-MENT FOR DOMES. THE SOULS ARE ALSO HUMAN LIKE IN APPEARANCE. THIS CIVILIZATION IS VERY OLD WITH ITS TURBULENCE LIKE OTHERS. HOWEVER, THEY LEARNED EARLY ON THE WAY TO THE LIGHT AND SPIRITUALITY IS THE ANSWER. THESE SOULS ARE ALSO A VERY LOVING, CARING, A KIND CIVILIZATION WHO SERVE AND HELP EACH OTHER. THERE ARE NO DARK OR GRAY ENTITIES ON THIS PLANET ONLY WHITE. AS THE OTHER SOULS ON THE OTHER PLANETS THEY HAVE HAD MANY VISITS TO *EARTH* IN THEIR SPACECRAFT WHICH ARE BASED AT THE BOTTOM OF THE OCEANS AT VARIOUS BASES AND DEPART

FROM THE OCEAN FLOOR. THESE SOULS LIVE AT LEAST 500 *EARTH* YEARS AND MORE. THEIR TECHNOLOGIES AGAIN ARE BEYOND THE COMPREHENSION OF HUMANS ON *EARTH*.

E – *YPUZA* (PRONOUNCED PUZA, THE Y IS SILENT)

MOTHER, TELL ME ABOUT THE PLANET **YPUZA.**

THIS PLANET SON, IS ONE OF MY FAVORITE PLANETS. IT IS VERY BEAUTIFUL WITH 4 RINGS AROUND IT AND 7 MOONS. IT IS IN THE GALAXY *RICONARY*. YOUR PLANET *EARTH* IS NOT AWARE OF THIS GALAXY. IT IS THE FURTHEST OF THE PLANETS DISCUSSED HERE FROM *EARTH*. THE PEOPLE ARE HUMAN LIKE AS *EARTH* INHABITANTS AND THEIR LIFE SPAN IS WELL OVER TWO THOUSAND YEARS. THEY ARE A HIGHLY ADVANCED CIVILIZATION. IT IS A LARGE PLANET WITH VAST OCEANS AND MAGNIFICENT MOUNTAINS. THE SOULS ON THIS PLANET NUMBER OVER 7 BILLION. THERE ARE NO DARK OR GRAY ENTITIES ON THIS PLANET ONLY WHITE ENTITIES WHO ARE HIGHLY EVOLVED SOULS IN SPIRIT AND LOVE. LONG AGO THEY DID HAVE A TURBULENT HISTORY BUT QUICKLY REALIZED THE WAY WAS THROUGH LOVE AND TAKING CARE OF EACH OTHER. THEY HAVE VISITED *EARTH* SEVERAL TIMES IN THE PAST AND ARE ALARMED AT THE DIRECTION *EARTH* HAS TAKEN.

2 – *MOTHER, WHY ARE ALL THE INHABITANTS OF THE PLANETS IN THE UNIVERSE HUMAN LIKE?*

BECAUSE, SON IT IS THE IMAGE OF FATHER AND I WHEN WE COME INTO PHYSICAL FORM FROM SPIRIT FORM. IT IS BEST TO HAVE CONSISTENCY OF PHYSICAL FORM. SOULS FEEL MORE COMFORTABLE WITH EACH OTHER IF THEY ALL ARE IN THE SAME FORM.

3 – MOTHER TELL ME ABOUT AREA 51 IN NEVADA AND HOW IT DEVELOPED?

SON, IT IS A SITE WHERE SOME OF THE SPACECRAFT FROM THE *ANDROMEDA* GALAXY LANDED. THERE WAS NO CRASH. THE SOULS FROM THE *ANDROMEDA* GALAXY USED THIS SITE TO BRANCH OUT AND EXPLORE ON *EARTH*. *ABTOURI* IS THE PLANET IN THE *ANDROMEDA* GALAXY. THE PLANET *ABTOURI* IS A VERY BEAUTIFUL PLANET WITH 4 RINGS AND 3 MOONS. THE TECHNOLOGY AND KNOWL-EDGE IS BEYOND THE COMPREHENSION OF *EARTH*.

THE SOULS FROM *ABTOURI* ARE ALL WHITE ENTITIES AND WANTED TO LEARN ABOUT *EARTH* BECAUSE THEY ARE CONCERNED AS THE REST OF THE UNIVERSE ON THE DI-RECTION *EARTH* IS GOING IN. THEY ARE HUMAN LIKE AS ALL THE OTHER INHABITANTS IN THE UNIVERSE. YOUR GOVERNMENT NOTICED THESE SPACECRAFT BECAUSE THEY CAME INTO THE THIRD DIMENSION, SO THEY COULD BE DETECTED. ATTEMPTS WERE MADE TO CAP-TURE THE SOULS AND SPACECRAFT FROM *ABTOURI* BUT THAT PROVED FUTILE BECAUSE THE TECHNOLOGICAL ADVANCEMENT IS BEYOND COMPREHENSION OF *EARTH*.

THE SPACECRAFT FROM *ABTOURI* ARE SMALL AND ARE

SAUCER SHAPED WITH ONLY A FEW SOULS PER CRAFT. THE ABTOURIANS, AS ALL SOULS IN THE UNIVERSE, COME AS LOVING NOT HOSTILE IN ANY MANNER.

YOUR GOVERNMENT SET UP AN AIRBASE THERE IN THE HOPES OF HAVING FURTHER CONTACT WITH THE ABTOURIANS. BECAUSE OF THE FEAR ANY SHARED KNOWLEDGE COULD BE USED AS AN ADVANTAGE IN WAR, NO CONTACT WAS MADE.

4 – *MOTHER, TELL ME ABOUT THE PYRAMIDS AND HOW THEY WERE BUILT.*

SON, THE PYRAMIDS WERE BUILT BY THE PEOPLE OF EGYPT WITH THE HELP OF AN ADVANCED CIVILIZATION IN THE UNIVERSE. AT THAT TIME ENGINEERING FEATS OF THIS NATURE WERE IMPOSSIBLE BY THE CULTURES OF *EARTH.*

THUS, VISITS OCCURRED BY A CIVILIZATION FROM THE *ANDROMEDA* GALAXY, FROM THE PLANET *PORTATORA.* A BEAUTIFUL PLANET OF WHITE ENTITIES WHO HELPED THE EGYPTIANS BUILD THE PYRAMIDS AND THE SPHINX. BY USING THE ENERGY OF CONSCIOUSNESS TO LIFT THE BLOCKS OF STONE, WHICH WERE CARVED BY THE EGYPTIANS; BY RELEASING THE DOWNWARD EFFECT OF GRAVITY. ADVICE WAS GIVEN TO THE EGYPTIANS ON THE ENGINEERING CHARACTERISTICS OF ALL THE PYRAMIDS.

THE *PORTATORIANS* COMMUNICATED WITH THE EGYPTIANS BY TELEPATHY. THE EGYPTIANS BEING VERY PRIMITIVE CONSIDERED THE *PORTATORIANS* GODS.

Mother, the *PORTATORIANS* controlled the energy of consciousness to release the downward effect of gravity, so these huge blocks of stones could be lifted and put in place.

CORRECT SON.

CHAPTER 15

THE GREAT BATTLE OF THE UNIVERSE

MOTHER SPEAKS TO ME, I, URA.

SON, YOU WERE SELECTED AT YOUR INCEPTION OF YOUR EMBRYO FORM FOR A SPECIAL PURPOSE. YOU ARE A PROTECTOR, A SPIRITUAL WARRIOR FOR JUSTICE AND GOOD. YOUR ROLE IS UNIQUE AND WAS DESIGNED FOR YOU BY MYSELF AND FATHER. YOU ARE NOT IN A GROUP OF HIGHLY EVOLVED SOULS. THERE IS ONLY YOU, NO GROUP. YOUR TASKS WERE DESIGNED FOR YOU TO BRING A BRIGHTER GREATER LIGHT TO THE UNIVERSE WHICH WILL BENEFIT ALL SOULS. THERE WILL BE A GREAT BATTLE AGAINST THE DARKNESS IN THE UNIVERSE. YOU WILL FIGHT FOR JUSTICE AND PROTECT AGAINST EVIL IN THE UNIVERSE. FATHER AND I SELECTED YOU FOR YOUR SOUL CHARACTERISTICS. WE KNEW LONG AGO A DARKNESS OF EVIL WOULD RISE IN THE UNIVERSE. THE LIGHT IN THE GREAT BATTLE REQUIRED A LEADER. WE SELECTED YOU.

THERE WILL BE MANY ANGELS AND WARRIOR SOULS YOU WILL LEAD IN THE GREAT BATTLE. THEY WILL BE YOUR BROTHERS IN ARMS. THE GREAT BATTLE WAS FORESEEN BY MYSELF AND FATHER LONG AGO AND WE NEEDED A SOUL TO LEAD THE WARRIORS OF THE LIGHT AND WE CHOSE YOU.

CHAPTER 16

HIDDEN

It usually always happens this way. I ask Mother a question and I just start writing. As she dictates to me. She just takes over the conversation. Then she just confirms what she told me with a Clairsentience blast, no doubt. Mother talks to me as I talk to you.

Well, it was different one evening in late April. I was watching TV sitting in the recliner chair with Klea and Mother just started to talk to me. Immediately, I knew she just wanted to talk. To clear her heart. Remember Mother and I have INSTANTANEOUS COMMUNICATION ON ALL LEVELS. It is amazing our bonds of communication. Mother says "Once you realized in the deep recesses of your mind that I was your Eternal Mother, our communication just 'skyrocketed' at every level of consciousness."

So I grabbed a pad and just started writing. Here is what she said to me that night. I did not ask questions that night. Mother just wanted to talk to me. I knew instantaneously she needed to clear her heart.

This is what Mother said to me that night in late April.

Father and I kept you HIDDEN, 'under the radar' through the ages. We made sure no attention was drawn to you. Yes son, we kept it, your real identity, quiet in the Universe. Only Father and I knew, through the ages.

That is why everybody was 'shocked' on The Other Sides throughout the inhabited planets of the Universe. No one knew, it had to be that way. Father and I could not allow you to be hurt, harmed in any way when you had all your incarnations. That would have been unbearable to have you hurt by The Darkness. That we could not allow. You were just too important to us and the Universe we created. The souls in the Universe need you now. It is time to return HOME for eternity to us, son.

We could not trust that something like this would ever 'leak out'. You are just too important. No one could know. Father and I are so anxious to get you HOME. We love you so much. You are such an exceptional soul.

You had to 'blend in'. We could never take the risk of you being 'singled out'. No attention could be drawn to you about who you really were. The wait is almost over now.

As Klea is listening to this sitting with me in the recliner chair she says **"Honey, what a story."** The only thing I can do is just listen in sheer amazement.

CHAPTER 17

JUST A REGULAR GUY

I am just a regular guy. Well at least I thought so. Spent my life in medicine and science. Grew up in the very hard environment of the Bronx, New York City. I was always 'it is what it is' kinda guy. A very 'down to earth guy'. A no nonsense guy. A very rational, analytical, objective person. Now all this happens, which began when my Felecia, or now I know as Klea returned to The Other Side for eternity.

Now what to make of all this? Why me? Do I sound 'nuts' to you? Look at these 100 questions I asked Mother God. Carefully read her answers. Now realistically could I even in any form of measurement come even close to the wisdom, understanding, and knowledge she expresses. This is 'so far above my pay grade' as they say. Sure, I can think of the questions but look carefully at these answers. "Come on, give me a break!!!"

This spiritual journey started Monday at 5:31 AM in the morning of November 5, 2018. What a way to start off the week. When my very beautiful, Klea, Felecia in this life returned home for all eternity. I would never in my wildest dreams conceive what has happened the last 30 months. If before our spiritual journey started someone would have said to me all this would happen, my simple response would have been "Have you totally lost your mind?" At times it is so surreal I question to myself is all this really happening? I have no idea where we go from here. I just am going along for the ride. What else can I do? I might as well enjoy it as much as possible. So much has happened in this journey. How in one's right mind can I reject it? On what grounds? Just to close my mind off, become the total blind mind, never to see or hear. Would I be so foolish to do something like that, to ignore all that has happened the last 30 months. Come on, I think, I have more intelligence than that.

This is the Trilogy of Klea and Ura's Spiritual Journey. Who knows what happens next? I certainly don't have a clue, any idea.

I only know one thing that is certain, is absolute for all eternity my intense, unshakable, unbreakable love for my Felecia, my Klea, will always be till the end of time in this Universe, whatever time that is. If there is such a thing as time.

Eternal love to you my beautiful Klea, from the regular guy.

CHAPTER 18

THE EPIPHANY MOMENT

The Epiphany moment as defined from Ancient Greek is an experience of a sudden and striking realization. This moment occurred the night of April 24, 2021. This 30-month journey from the very beginning was all about **THE KNOWLEDGE**. The Knowledge from our Co-Creators that had to be brought to this world into the light. All along this was the master design to bring **THE KNOWLEDGE** to the souls of this small planet of *Earth*, in the small *Orion Arm of the Milky Way Galaxy*.

This Epiphany Moment occurred to me as I was reading those answers to the many questions of the Universe, to marvel at the precise logic, to capture the insight, the essence of the meaning with a few words, the deep wisdom, the understanding of this Universe created by Mother and Father God in relation to this planet. The place our planet *Earth* holds in this vast Universe.

At the beginning of this Spiritual Journey over two years ago this is what it was all about from the very beginning. **THE KNOWLEDGE** revealed at the end. Hidden from me. This was why Klea had to return HOME when she did. It was all a universal plan designed by our Co-Creators. Remember the future has happened. The past is still happening. The cycle, the circle of no time.

It was about **THE KNOWLEDGE** all along, from the beginning. All this time. At the beginning of this journey I could not see, I was blinded by the pain and suffering. As the journey progressed I was obsessed by the communication with Klea on The Other Side, never thinking, never seeing that there may be a Master Plan of **THE KNOWLEDGE**, given to the souls of this small planet that has lost its way in the quest to see the light. Think of the magnitude of **THE KNOWLEDGE**. The deep depths of the repercussions of **THE KNOWLEDGE** to the billions of souls here struggling to understand their existence.

Where do we go from here? Will **THE KNOWLEDGE** be used for the greater good on *Earth?* Understanding now the nature of Good and Evil in the Universe, will it help the souls on this planet to prevail over evil? Will this planet succumb to The Darkness or walk into the brightness, the glow of The Light? Thus, now we wait for the Great Battle in the Universe to bring a new dawn to the Universe. To bring in hope the total victory of The Light over The Darkness. Will **THE KNOWLEDGE** be spread across the lands to be shared by the souls on this planet we call home, *Earth?*

I LOVE YOU MOTHER

I LOVE YOU SON

MOTHER WHEN I RETURN HOME

WE WILL BE A FAMILY

YOU AND FATHER

KLEA AND I

❦ NOTES

❦ NOTES

❦ NOTES

❧ NOTES

❦ NOTES

❦ NOTES

❦ NOTES

❧ NOTES

❦ NOTES

❧ NOTES

❦ NOTES

Made in the USA
Middletown, DE
07 June 2021